# MARGOT ASQUITH

## AN AUTOBIOGRAPHY

### IN TWO VOLUMES

WITH TWENTY-FOUR ILLUSTRATIONS
AND NUMEROUS REPRODUCTIONS OF
ORIGINAL DRAWINGS

5. Verily every man at his best state is altogether vanity.

6. Surely every man walketh in a vain shew: surely they are disquieted in vain: he heapeth up riches, and knoweth not who shall gather them.

7. And now, Lord, what wait I for? my hope is in Thee.

MARGOT, LEADING SPIRIT OF THE SOULS
(PENCIL DRAWING BY THE MARCHIONESS
OF GRANBY, DUCHESS OF RUTLAND)

# MARGOT ASQUITH
## AN AUTOBIOGRAPHY

VOLUME TWO

NEW YORK
GEORGE H. DORAN COMPANY

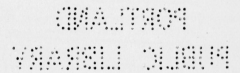

# CONTENTS OF
# VOLUME TWO

### CHAPTER I

# CONTENTS

# ILLUSTRATIONS OF
# VOLUME TWO

[ vii ]

# ILLUSTRATIONS

# MARGOT ASQUITH
## AN AUTOBIOGRAPHY

# MARGOT ASQUITH
## AN AUTOBIOGRAPHY

## CHAPTER I

THE SOULS—LORD CURZON'S POEM AND DINNER
PARTY AND WHO WERE THERE—MARGOT'S IN-
VENTORY OF THE GROUP—TILT WITH THE LATE
LADY LONDONDERRY—VISIT TO TENNYSON; HIS
CONTEMPT FOR CRITICS; HIS HABIT OF LIVING—
J. K. S. NOT A SOUL—MARGOT'S FRIENDSHIP
WITH JOHN ADDINGTON SYMONDS; HIS PRAISE
OF MARIE BASHKIRTSEFF

NO one ever knew how it came about that I and
my particular friends were called "the Souls."
The origin of our grouping together I have already
explained: we saw more of one another than we
should probably have done had my sister Laura
Lyttelton lived, because we were in mourning and
did not care to go out in general society; but why
we were called "Souls" I do not know.

The fashionable—what was called the "smart

set"—of those days centred round the Prince of Wales, afterwards King Edward VII., and had Newmarket for its head-quarters. As far as I could see, there was more exclusiveness in the racing world than I had ever observed among the Souls; and the first and only time I went to Newmarket the welcome extended to me by the shrewd and select company there made me feel exactly like an alien.

We did not play bridge or baccarat and our rather intellectual and literary after-dinner games were looked upon as pretentious.

Arthur Balfour—the most distinguished of the Souls and idolised by every set in society—was the person who drew the enemy's fire. He had been well known before he came among us and it was considered an impertinence on our part to make him play pencil-games or be our intellectual guide and critic. Nearly all the young men in my circle were clever and became famous; and the women, although not more intelligent, were less worldly than their fashionable contemporaries and many of them both good to be with and distinguished to look at.

What interests me most on looking back now at

those ten years is the loyalty, devotion and fidelity which we showed to one another and the pleasure which we derived from friendships that could not have survived a week had they been accompanied by gossip, mocking, or any personal pettiness. Most of us had a depth of feeling and moral and religious ambition which are entirely lacking in the clever young men and women of to-day. Our after-dinner games were healthier and more inspiring than theirs. "Breaking the news," for instance, was an entertainment that had a certain vogue among the younger generation before the war. It consisted of two people acting together and conveying to their audience various ways in which they would receive the news of the sudden death of a friend or a relation and was considered extraordinarily funny; it would never have amused any of the Souls. The modern habit of pursuing, detecting and exposing what was ridiculous in simple people and the unkind and irreverent manner in which slips were made material for epigram were unbearable to me. This school of thought—which the young group called "anticant"—encouraged hard sayings and light doings, which would have profoundly shocked the most frivolous among us.

[13]

Brilliance of a certain kind may bring people together for amusement, but it will not keep them
together for long; and the young, hard pre-war
group that I am thinking of was short-lived.

The present Lord Curzon* also drew the enemy's
fire and was probably more directly responsible for
the name of the Souls than any one.

He was a conspicuous young man of ability,
with a ready pen, a ready tongue, an excellent sense
of humour in private life and intrepid social bold-
ness. He had appearance more than looks, a keen,
lively face, with an expression of enamelled self-
assurance. Like every young man of exceptional
promise, he was called a prig. The word was so
misapplied in those days that, had I been a clever
young man, I should have felt no confidence in
myself till the world had called me a prig. He
was a remarkably intelligent person in an exceptional generation. He had ambition and—what he
claimed for himself in a brilliant description—
"middle-class method"; and he added to a kindly
feeling for other people a warm corner for himself.
Some of my friends thought his contemporaries in
the House of Commons, George Wyndham and

*Earl Curzon of Kedleston.

[14]

THE RIGHT HONORABLE ARTHUR JAMES BALFOUR
AS HE APPEARED IN THE HOUSE OF COMMONS
DURING THE 80's

Harry Cust, would go farther, as the former promised more originality and the latter was a finer scholar, but I always said—and have a record of it in my earliest diaries—that George Curzon would easily outstrip his rivals. He had two incalculable advantages over them: he was chronically industrious and self-sufficing; and, though Oriental in his ideas of colour and ceremony, with a poor sense of proportion, and a childish love of fine people, he was never self-indulgent. He neither ate, drank nor smoked too much and left nothing to chance.

No one could turn with more elasticity from work to play than George Curzon; he was a first-rate host and boon companion and showed me and mine a steady and sympathetic love over a long period of years. Even now, if I died, although he belongs to the more conventional and does not allow himself to mix with people of opposite political parties, he would write my obituary notice.

At the time of which I am telling, he was threatened with lung trouble and was ordered to Switzerland by his doctors. We were very unhappy and assembled at a farewell banquet, to which he entertained us in the Bachelors' Club, on the 10th of July, 1889. We found a poem welcoming us

[15]

on our chairs, when we sat down to dinner, in which we were all honourably and categorically mentioned. Some of our critics called us "the Gang"—to which allusion is made here—but we were ultimately known as the Souls.

This famous dinner and George's poem caused a lot of fun and friction, jealousy, curiosity and endless discussion. It was followed two years later by another dinner given by the same host to the same guests and in the same place, on the 9th of July, 1891.

The repetition of this dinner was more than the West End of London could stand; and I was the object of much obloquy. I remember dining with Sir Stanley and Lady Clarke to meet King Edward—then Prince of Wales—when my hostess said to me in a loud voice, across the table:

"There were some clever people in the world, you know, before you were born, Miss Tennant!"

Feeling rather nettled, I replied:

"Please don't pick me out, Lady Clarke, as if I alone were responsible for the stupid ones among whom we find ourselves to-day."

Having no suspicion of other people, I was seldom on the defensive and did not mean to be rude, but I was young and intolerant.

This was George Curzon's poem:

### 10th JULY, 1889.

Ho! list to a lay
Of that company gay,
Compounded of gallants and graces,
Who gathered to dine,
In the year '89,
In a haunt that in Hamilton Place is.

There, there where they met,
And the banquet was set
At the bidding of GEORGIUS CURZON;
Brave youth! 'tis his pride,
When he errs, that the side
Of respectable licence he errs on.

Around him that night—
Was there e'er such a sight?
Souls sparkled and spirits expanded;
For of them critics sang,
That tho' christened the Gang,
By a spiritual link they were banded.

Souls and spirits, no doubt
But neither without
Fair visible temples to dwell in!
E'en your image divine
Must be girt with a shrine,
For the pious to linger a spell in.

# MARGOT ASQUITH

There was seen at that feast
Of this band, the High Priest,
The heart that to all hearts is nearest;
Him may nobody steal
From the true Common weal,
Tho' to each is dear ARTHUR[1] the dearest.

America lends,
Nay, she gives when she sends
Such treasures as HARRY[2] and DAISY[2];
Tho' many may yearn,
None but HARRY can turn
That sweet little head of hers crazy.

There was much-envied STRATH[3]
With the lady[3] who hath
Taught us all what may life be at twenty;
Of pleasure a taste,
Of duty no waste,
Of gentle philosophy plenty.

KITTY DRUMMOND[4] was there—
Where was LAWRENCE,[4] oh! where?—
And my Lord[5] and my Lady GRANBY[5];
Is there one of the Gang
Has not wept at the pang
That he never can VIOLET's man be?

From WILTON, whose streams
Murmur sweet in our dreams,

[1] The Right Hon. A. J. Balfour.
[2] Mr. and Mrs. White.
[3] The Duke and Duchess of Sutherland.
[4] Col. and Mrs. L. Drummond.
[5] Now the Duke and Duchess of Rutland.

[18]

# AN AUTOBIOGRAPHY

Come the Earl[6] and his Countess[6] together;
 In her spirit's proud flights
 We are whirled to the heights,
He sweetens our stay in the nether.

 Dear Evan[7] was there,
 The first choice of the fair,
To all but himself very gentle!
 And Ashridge's lord [8]
 Most insufferably bored
With manners and modes Oriental.

 The Shah, I would bet,
 In the East never met
Such a couple as him and his consort.[8]
 If the Horners[9] you add,
 That a man must be mad
Who complains that the Gang is a wrong sort.

 From kindred essay
 Lady Mary[10] to-day
Should have beamed on a world that adores her.
 Of her spouse[10] debonair
 No woman has e'er
Been able to say that he bores her.

 Next Bingy [11] escorts
 His dear wife,[11] to our thoughts
Never lost, though withdrawn from our vision,

[6] Earl and Countess of Pembroke.
[7] Hon. Evan Charteris.
[8] Earl and Countess Brownlow.
[9] Sir J. and Lady Horner.
[10] Lord and Lady Elcho (now Earl and Countess of Wemyss).
[11] Lord and Lady Wenlock.

While of late she has shown
That of spirit alone
Was not fashioned that fair composition.

No, if humour we count,
The original fount
Must to HUGO be ceded in freehold,
Tho' of equal supplies
In more subtle disguise
Old GODFREY[12] has far from a wee hold!

MRS. EDDY [13] has come
And we all shall be dumb
When we hear what a lovely voice Emmy's is;
SPENCER,[14] too, would show what
He can do, were it not
For that cursed laryngeal Nemesis.

At no distance away
Behold ALAN[15] display
That smile that is found so upsetting;
And EDGAR[16] in bower,
In statecraft, in power,
The favourite first in the betting.

Here a trio we meet,
Whom you never will beat,
Tho' wide you may wander and far go;
From what wonderful art

[12] Mr. Godfrey Webb.
[13] The Hon. Mrs. E. Bourke.
[14] The Hon. Spencer Lyttelton.
[15] The Hon. Alan Charteris.
[16] Sir E. Vincent (now Lord D'Abernon).

# AN AUTOBIOGRAPHY

Of that Gallant Old Bart.,
Sprang CHARTY and LUCY and MARGOT?

To LUCY[17] he gave
The wiles that enslave,
Heart and tongue of an angel to CHARTY[18];
To MARGOT[19] the wit
And the wielding of it,
That make her the joy of a party.

LORD TOMMY[20] is proud
That to CHARTY he vowed
The graces and gifts of a true man.
And proud are the friends
Of ALFRED,[21] who blends
The athlete, the hero, the woman!

From the Gosford preserves
Old ST. JOHN[22] deserves
Great praise for a bag such as HILDA[22];
True worth she esteemed,
Overpowering he deemed
The subtle enchantment that filled her.

Very dear are the pair,
He so strong, she so fair,
Renowned as the TAPLOVITE WINNIES;
Ah! he roamed far and wide,

[17] Mrs. Graham Smith.
[18] Lady Ribblesdale.
[19] Mrs. Asquith.
[20] Lord Ribblesdale.
[21] The Hon. Alfred Lyttelton.
[22] The Hon. St. John Brodrick (now Earl of Midleton) and Lady Hilda Brodrick.

Till in ETTY[23] he spied
A treasure more golden than guineas.

Here is DOLL[24] who has taught
Us that "words conceal thought"
In his case is a fallacy silly;
    HARRY CUST[25] could display
    Scalps as many, I lay,
From Paris as in Piccadilly.

But some there were too—
Thank the Lord they were few!
Who were bidden to come and who could not:
    Was there one of the lot,
    Ah! I hope there was not,
Looked askance at the bidding and would not.

The brave LITTLE EARL[26]
Is away, and his pearl-
Laden spouse, the imperial GLADYS[26];
    By that odious gout
    Is LORD COWPER[27] knocked out.
And the wife[27] who his comfort and aid is.

MISS BETTY's engaged,
And we all are enraged
That the illness of SIBELL's[28] not over;
    GEORGE WYNDHAM[29] can't sit

[23] Mr. and Mrs. Willy Grenfell (now Lord and Lady Desborough).
[24] Mr. A. G. Liddell.
[25] Mr. Harry Cust.
[26] Earl and Countess de Grey.
[27] Earl and Countess Cowper.
[28] Countess Grosvenor.
[29] The late Right Hon. George Wyndham.

[22]

At our banquet of wit,
Because he is standing at Dover.

But we ill can afford
To dispense with the Lord
Of WADDESDON[30] and ill HARRY CHAPLIN[31];
Were he here, we might shout
As again he rushed out
From the back of that "d—d big sapling."

We have lost LADY GAY[32]
'Tis a price hard to pay
For that Shah and his appetite greedy;
And alas! we have lost—
At what ruinous cost!—
The charms of the brilliant MISS D.D.[33]

But we've got in their place,
For a gift of true grace,
VIRGINIA's marvellous daughter.[34]
Having conquered the States,
She's been blown by the Fates
To conquer us over the water.

Now this is the sum
Of all those who have come
Or ought to have come to that banquet.
Then call for the bowl,
Flow spirit and soul,
Till midnight not one of you can quit!

[30] Baron Ferdinand de Rothschild.
[31] Now Viscount Chaplin.
[32] Lady Windsor (now Marchioness of Plymouth).
[33] Miss E. Balfour (Widow of the Hon. Alfred Lyttelton).
[34] Mrs. Chanler, the American novelist (now Princess Troubetzkoy).

And blest by the Gang
Be the Rhymester who sang
Their praises in doggrel appalling;
More now were a sin—
Ho, waiters, begin!
Each soul for consommé is calling!

. . . . . . .

For my own and the children's interest I shall
try, however imperfectly, to make a descriptive
inventory of some of the Souls mentioned in this
poem and of some of my friends who were not.

Gladstone's secretary, Sir Algernon West,* and
Godfrey Webb had both loved Laura and corresponded with her till she died and they spent all
their holidays at Glen. I never remember the
time when Algy West was not getting old and
did not say he wanted to die; but, although he is
ninety, he is still young, good-looking and—what
is even more remarkable—a strong Liberal. He
was never one of the Souls, but he was a faithful
and loving early friend of ours.

Mr. Godfrey Webb was the doyen of the Souls.
He was as intimate with my brothers and parents
as he was with my sisters and self. Godfrey—
or Webber as some called him—was not only a man

*The Right Hon. Sir Algernon West.

of parts, but had a peculiar flavour of his own: he had the sense of humour and observation of a memoirist and his wit healed more than it cut. For hours together he would poke about the country with a dog, a gun and a cigar, perfectly independent and self-sufficing, whether engaged in sport, repartee, or literature. He wrote and published for private circulation a small book of poems and made the Souls famous by his proficiency at all our pencil-games. It would be unwise to quote verses or epigrams that depend so much upon the occasion and the environment. Only a George Meredith can sustain a preface boasting of his heroine's wit throughout the book, but I will risk one example of Godfrey Webb's quickness. He took up a newspaper one morning in the dining-room at Glen and, reading that a Mr. Pickering Phipps had broken his leg on rising from his knees at prayer, he immediately wrote this couplet:

> On bended knees, with fervent lips,
> Wrestled with Satan Pickering Phipps,
> But when for aid he ceased to beg,
> The wily devil broke his leg!

He spent every holiday with us and I do not think he ever missed being with us on the anniversary of Laura's death, whether I was at home or abroad. He was a man in a million, the last of the wits, and I miss him every day of my life.

.  .  .  .  .  .  .

Lord Midleton*—better known as St. John Brodrick—was my first friend of interest; I knew him two years before I met Arthur Balfour or any of the Souls. He came over to Glen while he was staying with neighbours of ours.

I wired to him not long ago to congratulate him on being made an Earl and asked him in what year it was that he first came to Glen; this is his answer:

*Jan.* 12th, 1920.

DEAREST MARGOT,

I valued your telegram of congratulation the more that I know you and Henry (who has given so many and refused all) attach little value to titular distinctions. Indeed, it is the only truly democratic trait about *you*, except a general love of H· manity, which has always put you on the side of the feeble. I am relieved to hear you have chosen such a reliable man as Crewe—with his literary gifts—to be the only person to read your autobiography.

My visit to Glen in R——y's company was October, 1880, when you were sixteen. You and Laura flashed like meteors on to a dreary scene of

* The Right Hon. the Earl of Midleton, of Peper, Harow, Godalming.

empty seats at the luncheon table (the shooting party didn't come in) and filled the room with light, electrified the conversation and made old R——y falter over his marriage vows within ten minutes. From then onwards, you have always been the most loyal and indulgent of friends, forgetting no one as you rapidly climbed to fame, and were raffled for by all parties—from Sandringham to the crossing-sweeper.

Your early years will sell the book.

Bless you.

ST. JOHN.

St. John Midleton was one of the rare people who tell the truth. Some people do not lie, but have no truth to tell; others are too agreeable—or too frightened—and lie; but the majority are indifferent: they are the spectators of life and feel no responsibility either towards themselves or their neighbour.

He was fundamentally humble, truthful and one of the few people I know who are truly loyal and who would risk telling me, or any one he loved, before confiding to an inner circle faults which both he and I think might be corrected. I have had a long experience of inner circles and am constantly reminded of the Spanish proverb, "Remember your friend has a friend." I think you

[27]

should either leave the room when those you love
are abused or be prepared to warn them of what
people are thinking. This is, as I know to my cost,
an unpopular view of friendship, but neither St.
John nor I would think it loyal to join in the
laughter or censure of a friend's folly.

Arthur Balfour himself—the most persistent of
friends—remarked laughingly:

"St. John pursues us with his malignant
fidelity." *

This was only a coloured way of saying that
Midleton had none of the detachment commonly
found among friends; but, as long as we are not
merely responsible for our actions to the police, so
long must I believe in trying to help those we love.

St. John has the same high spirits and keenness
now that he had then and the same sweetness and
simplicity. There are only a few women whose
friendships have remained as loving and true to me
since my girlhood as his—Lady Horner, Miss
Tomlinson,† Lady Desborough, Mrs. Montgomery, Lady Wemyss and Lady Bridges‡—but ever
since we met in 1880 he has taken an interest in

---

* The word *malignity* was obviously used in the sense of the French
*malin.*
† Miss May Tomlinson, of Rye.
‡ Lady Bridges, wife of General Sir Tom Bridges.

me and all that concerns me. He was much
maligned when he was Secretary of State for War
and bore it without blame or bitterness. He had
infinite patience, intrepid courage and a high sense
of duty; these combined to give him a better place
in the hearts of men than in the fame of newspapers.

His first marriage was into a family who were
incapable of appreciating his particular quality and
flavour; even his mother-in-law—a dear friend of
mine—never understood him and was amazed when
I told her that her son-in-law was worth all of her
children put together, because he had more nature
and more enterprise. I have tested St. John now
for many years and never found him wanting.

. . . . . . .

Lord Pembroke* and George Wyndham were
the handsomest of the Souls. Pembroke was the
son of Sidney Herbert, famous as Secretary of
State for War during the Crimea. I met him
first the year before I came out. Lord Kitchener's
friend, Lady Waterford—sister to the present
Duke of Beaufort—wrote to my mother asking if
Laura could dine with her, as she had been thrown
over at the last minute and wanted a young

* George, 13th Earl of Pembroke.

woman. As my sister was in the country, my mother sent me. I sat next to Arthur Balfour; Lord Pembroke was on the other side, round the corner of the table; and I remember being intoxicated with my own conversation and the manner in which I succeeded in making Balfour and Pembroke join in. I had no idea who the splendid stranger was. He told me several years later that he had sent round a note in the middle of that dinner to Blanchie Waterford, asking her what the name of the girl with the red heels was, and that, when he read her answer, "Margot Tennant," it conveyed nothing to him. This occurred in 1881 and was for me an eventful evening. Lord Pembroke was one of the four best-looking men I ever saw: the others, as I have already said, were the late Earl of Wemyss, Mr. Wilfrid Blunt—whose memoirs have been rceently published—and Lord D'Abernon.* He was six foot four, but his face was even more conspicuous than his height. There was Russian blood in the Herbert family and he was the eldest brother of the beautiful Lady Ripon. † He married Lady Gertrude Talbot,

*Our Ambassador in Berlin.
†The late wife of the present Marquis of Ripon.

daughter of the twentieth Earl of Shrewsbury and Talbot, who was nearly as fine to look at as he himself. He told me among other things at that dinner that he had known Disraeli and had been promised some minor post in his government, but had been too ill at the time to accept it. This developed into a discussion on politics and Peeblesshire, leading up to our county neighbours; he asked me if I knew Lord Elcho,* of whose beauty Ruskin had written, and who owned property in my county.

"Elcho," said he, "always expected to be invited to join the government, but I said to Dizzy, 'Elcho is an impossible politician; he has never understood the meaning of party government and looks upon it as dishonest for even three people to attempt to modify their opinions sufficiently to come to an agreement, leave alone a Cabinet! He is an egotist!' To which Disraeli replied, 'Worse than that! He is an Elchoist!' "

Although Lord Pembroke's views on all subjects were remarkably wide—as shown by the book he published called *Roots*—he was a Conservative. We formed a deep friendship and wrote to one

*The father of the present Earl of Wemyss and March.

another till he died a few years after my marriage. In one of his letters to me he added this postscript:

Keep the outer borders of your heart's sweet garden free from garish flowers and wild and careless weeds, so that when your fairy godmother turns the Prince's footsteps your way he may not, distrusting your nature or his own powers, and only half-guessing at the treasure within, tear himself reluctantly away, and pass sadly on, without perhaps your ever knowing that he had been near.

This, I imagine, gave a correct impression of me as I appeared to some people. "Garish flowers" and "wild and careless weeds" describe my lack of pruning; but I am glad George Pembroke put them on the "outer," not the inner, borders of my heart.

In the tenth verse of Curzon's poem, allusion is made to Lady Pembroke's conversation, which though not consciously pretentious, provoked considerable merriment. She "stumbled upwards into vacuity," to quote my dear friend Sir Walter Raleigh.

There is no one left to-day at all like George Pembroke. His combination of intellectual temperament, gregariousness, variety of tastes—yachting, art, sport and literature—his beauty of person and hospitality to foreigners made him the distinguished centre of any company. His first present to me was Butcher and Lang's translation of the *Odyssey*, in which he wrote on the fly-leaf, "To Margot, who most reminds me of Homeric days, 1884," and his last was his wedding present, a diamond dagger, which I always wear close to my heart.

. . . . . .

Among the Souls, Milly Sutherland,[1] Lady Windsor[2] and Lady Granby[3] were the women whose looks I admired most. Lady Brownlow,[4] mentioned in verse eleven, was Lady Pembroke's handsome sister and a famous Victorian beauty. Lady Granby—the Violet of verse nine, Gladys Ripon[5] and Lady Windsor (alluded to as Lady Gay in verse twenty-eight), were all women of arresting appearance: Lady Brownlow, a Roman coin; Violet Rutland, a Burne-Jones Medusa; Gladys Ripon, a court lady; Gay Windsor, an Italian Primitive and Milly Sutherland, a Scotch ballad. Betty Montgomery was a brilliant girl and

[1] The Dowager Duchess of Sutherland.
[2] The present Countess of Plymouth.
[3] The present Duchess of Rutland.
[4] Countess Brownlow, who died a few years ago.
[5] My friend Lady de Grey.

the only unmarried woman, except Mrs. Lyttelton, among us. She was the daughter of Sir Henry Ponsonby, Queen Victoria's famous private secretary, and one of the strongest Liberals I ever met. Her sister Maggie, though socially uncouth, had a touch of her father's genius; she said of a court prelate to me one day at Windsor Castle:

"There goes God's butler!"

It was through Betty and Maggie Ponsonby that I first met my beloved friend, Lady Desborough. Though not as good-looking as the beauties I have catalogued, nor more intellectual than Lady Horner or Lady Wemyss, Lady Desborough was the cleverest of us. Her flavour was more delicate, her social sensibility finer; and she added to chronic presence of mind undisguised effrontery. I do not suppose she was ever unconscious in her life, but she had no self-pity and no egotism. She was not an artist in any way: music, singing, flowers, painting and colour left her cold. She was not a game-player nor was she sporting and she never invested in parlour tricks; yet she created more fun for other people than anybody. She was a woman of genius, who, if subtly and accurately described, either in her mode of life, her charm, wits or character, would have made the fortune of any novelist. To an outsider she might—like all over-agreeable *femmes du monde*—give an impression of light metal, but this would be misleading. Etty Desborough was fundamentally sound, and the truest friend that ever lived. Possessed of social and moral *sang-froid* of a high order, she was too elegant to fall into the trap of the candid friend, but nevertheless she could, when asked, give both counsel and judgment with the sympathy of a man and the wisdom of a god. She was the first person that I sought and that I would still seek if I were unhappy, because her genius lay in a penetrating understanding of the human heart and a determination to redress the balance of life's unhappiness. Etty and I attracted the same people. She married Willy Grenfell,* a man to whom I was much attached and a British gladiator capable of challenging the world in boating and boxing.

Of their soldier sons, Julian and Billy, I cannot write. They and their friends, Edward Horner, Charles Lister and Raymond Asquith all fell in the war. They haunt my heart; I can see them in

*Lord Desborough of Taplow Court.

front of me now, eternal sentinels of youth and manliness.

In spite of a voracious appetite for enjoyment and an expert capacity in entertaining, Etty Desborough was perfectly happy either alone with her family or alone with her books and could endure, with enviable patience, cold ugly country-seats and fashionable people. I said of her when I first knew her that she ought to have lived in the days of the great King's mistresses. I would have gone to her if I were sad, but never if I were guilty. Most of us have asked ourselves at one time or another whom we would go to if we had done a wicked thing; and the interesting part of this question is that in the answer you will get the best possible indication of human nature. Many have said to me, "I would go to So-and-so, because they would understand my temptation and make allowances for me"; but the majority would choose the confidante most competent to point to the way of escape. Etty Desborough would be that confidante.

She had neither father nor mother, but was brought up by two prominent and distinguished members of the Souls, my life-long and beloved friends, Lord and Lady Cowper of Panshanger, now, alas, both dead. Etty had eternal youth and was alive to everything in life except its irony.

If for health or for any other reason I had been separated from my children when they were young, I would as soon have confided them to the love of Etty and Willy Desborough as to any of my friends.

. . . . . . .

To illustrate the jealousy and friction which the Souls caused, I must relate a conversational scrap I had at this time with Lady Londonderry,* which caused some talk among our critics.

She was a beautiful woman, a little before my day, happy, courageous and violent, with a mind which clung firmly to the obvious. Though her nature was impulsive and kind, she was not forgiving. One day she said to me with pride:

"I am a good friend and a bad enemy. No kiss-and-make-friends about me, my dear!"

I have often wondered since, as I did then, what the difference between a good and a bad enemy is.

She was not so well endowed intellectually as her rival Lady de Grey, but she had a stronger will and was of sounder temperament.

There was nothing wistful, reflective or retiring

*The late Marchioness of Londonderry.

about Lady Londonderry. She was keen and vivid, but crude and impenitent.

We were accused *entre autres* of being conceited and of talking about books which we had not read, a habit which I have never had the temerity to acquire. John Addington Symonds—an intimate friend of mine—had brought out a book of essays, which were not very good and caused no sensation.

One night, after dinner, I was sitting in a circle of fashionable men and women—none of them particularly intimate with me—when Lady Londonderry opened the talk about books. Hardly knowing her, I entered with an innocent zest into the conversation. I was taken in by her mention of Symonds' *Studies in Italy,* and thought she must be literary. Launching out upon style, I said there was a good deal of rubbish written about it, but it was essential that people should write simply. At this some one twitted me with our pencil-game of "Styles" and asked me if I thought I should know the author from hearing a casual passage read out aloud from one of their books. I said that some writers would be easy to recognise—such as Meredith, Carlyle, De Quincey or Browning—but that when it came to others—men like Scott or Froude, for instance—I should not be so sure of myself. At this there was an outcry: Froude, having the finest style in the world, ought surely to be easily recognised! I was quite ready to believe that some of the company had made a complete study of Froude's style, but I had not. I said that I could not be sure, because his writing was too smooth and perfect, and that, when I read him, I felt as if I was swallowing arrow-root. This shocked them profoundly and I added that, unless I were to stumble across a horseman coming over a hill, or something equally fascinating, I should not even be sure of recognising Scott's style. This scandalised the company. Lady Londonderry then asked me if I admired Symonds' writing. I told her I did not, although I liked some of his books. She seemed to think that this was a piece of swagger on my part and, after disagreeing with a lofty shake of her head, said in a challenging manner:

"I should be curious to know, Miss Tennant, what you have read by Symonds!"

Feeling I was being taken on, I replied rather chillily:

"Oh, the usual sort of thing!"

Lady Londonderry, visibly irritated and with

the confident air of one who has a little surprise in store for the company, said:

"Have you by any chance looked at *Essays, Suggestive and Speculative?*"

MARGOT: "Yes, I've read them all."

LADY LONDONDERRY: "Really! Do you not approve of them?"

MARGOT: "Approve? I don't know what you mean."

LADY LONDONDERRY: "Do you not think the writing beautiful . . . the style, I mean?"

MARGOT: "I think they are all very bad, but then I don't admire Symonds' style."

LADY LONDONDERRY: "I am afraid you have not read the book."

This annoyed me; I saw the company were enchanted with their spokeswoman, but I thought it unnecessarily rude and more than foolish.

I looked at her calmly and said:

"I am afraid, Lady Londonderry, you have not read the preface. The book is dedicated to me. Symonds was a friend of mine and I was staying at Davos at the time he was writing those essays. He was rash enough to ask me to read one of them in manuscript and write whatever I thought upon

[40]

the margin. This I did, but he was offended by something I scribbled. I was so surprised at his minding that I told him he was never to show me any of his unpublished work again, at which he forgave me and dedicated the book to me."

After this flutter I was not taken on by fashionable ladies about books.

. . . . . . .

Lady Londonderry never belonged to the Souls, but her antagonist, Lady de Grey, was one of its chief ornaments and my friend. She was a luxurious woman of great beauty, with perfect manners and a moderate sense of duty. She was the last word in refinement, perception and charm. There was something septic in her nature and I heard her say one day that the sound of the cuckoo made her feel ill; but, although she was not lazy and seldom idle, she never developed her intellectual powers or sustained herself by reading or study of any kind. She had not the smallest sense of proportion and, if anything went wrong in her entertainments—cold plates, a flat *soufflé,* or some one throwing her over for dinner—she became almost impotent from agitation, only excusable if it had been some great public disaster. She and Mr. Harry Higgins—an exceptionally clever and devoted friend of mine—having revived the opera, Bohemian society became her hobby; but a tenor in the country or a dancer on the lawn are not really wanted; and, although she spent endless time  at Covent Garden and achieved considerable success, restlessness devoured her. While receiving the adoration of a small but influential circle, she appeared to me to have tried everything to no purpose and, in spite of an experience which queens and actresses, professionals and amateurs might well have envied, she remained embarrassed by herself, fluid, brilliant and uneasy. The personal nobility with which she worked her hospital in the Great War years brought her peace.

. . . . . . .

Frances Horner* was more like a sister to me than any one outside my own family. I met her when she was Miss Graham and I was fourteen. She was a leader in what was called the high art William Morris School and one of the few girls who ever had a salon in London.

I was deeply impressed by her appearance. it was the fashion of the day to wear the autumn desert in your hair and "soft shades" of Liberty velveteen; but it was neither the unusualness of her

*Lady Horner, of Mells, Frome.

clothes nor the sight of Burne-Jones at her feet and Ruskin at her elbow that struck me most, but what Charty's little boy, Tommy Lister, called her "ghost eyes" and the nobility of her countenance.

There may be women as well endowed with heart, head, temper and temperament as Frances Horner, but I have only met a few: Lady de Vesci (whose niece, Cynthia, married our poet-son, Herbert), Lady Betty Balfour* and my daughter Elizabeth. With most women the impulse to crab is greater than to praise and grandeur of character is surprisingly lacking in them; but Lady Horner comprises all that is best in my sex.

Mary Wemyss was one of the most distinguished of the Souls and was as wise as she was just, truthful, tactful, and generous. She might have been a great influence, as indeed she was always a great pleasure, but she was both physically and mentally badly equipped for coping with life and spent and wasted more time than was justifiable on plans which could have been done by any good servant. It would not have mattered the endless discussion whether the brougham fetching one part of the family from one station and a bus fetching another part

*Sister of the Earl of Lytton and wife of Mr. Gerald Balfour.

of it from another interfered with a guest catching a five or a five-to-five train—which could or could not be stopped—if one could have been quite sure that Mary Wemyss needed her friend so much that another opportunity would be given for an intimate interchange of confidences; but plan-weaving blinds people to a true sense of proportion and my beloved Mary never had enough time for any of us. She is the only woman I know or have ever known without smallness or touchiness of any kind. Her *juste milieu,* if a trifle becalmed, amounts to genius; and I was—and still am—more interested in her moral, social and intellectual opinions than in most of my friends'. Some years ago I wrote this in my diary about her:

"Mary is generally a day behind the fair and will only hear of my death from the man behind the counter who is struggling to clinch her over a collar for her chow."

.    .    .    .    .    .    .

One of the less prominent of the Souls was my friend, Lionel Tennyson.* He was the second son of the poet and was an official in the India Office. He had an untidy appearance, a black beard and

*Brother of the present Lord Tennyson.

no manners. He sang German beer-songs in a lusty voice and wrote good verses.

He sent me many poems, but I think these two are the best. The first was written to me on my twenty-first birthday, before the Souls came into existence:

What is a single flower when the world is white
    with may?
What is a gift to one so rich, a smile to one so gay?
What is a thought to one so rich in the loving
    thoughts of men?
How should I hope because I sigh that you will
    sigh again?
        Yet when you see my gift, you may
        (Ma bayadère aux yeux de jais)
        Think of me once to-day.


Think of me as you will, dear girl, if you will let
    me be
Somewhere enshrined within the fane of your pure
    memory;
Think of your poet as of one who only thinks of
    you,
That you *are* all his thought, that he were happy
    if he knew—
        You *did* receive his gift, and say
        (Ma bayadère aux yeux de jais)
        "He thinks of me to-day."

[45]

And this is the second:

> She drew me from my cosy seat,
> She drew me to her cruel feet,
> She whispered, "Call me Sally!"
> I lived upon her smile, her sigh,
> Alas, you fool, I knew not I
> Was only her *pis-aller*.

> The jade! she knew her business well,
> She made each hour a heaven or hell,
> For she could coax and rally;
> She was *so* loving, frank and kind,
> That no suspicion crost my mind
> That I was her *pis-aller*.

> My brother says "I told you so!
> Her conduct was not *comme il faut*,
> But strictly *comme il fallait;*
> She swore that she was fond and true;
> No doubt she was, poor girl, but you
> Were only her *pis-aller*."

He asked me what I would like him to give me for a birthday present, and I said:

"If you want to give me pleasure, take me down to your father's country house for a Saturday to Monday."

This Lionel arranged; and he and I went down to Aldworth, Haslemere, together from London.

[46]

While we were talking in the train, a distinguished old lady got in. She wore an ample black satin skirt, small black satin slippers in goloshes, a sable tippet and a large, picturesque lace bonnet. She did not appear to be listening to our conversation, because she was reading with an air of concentration; but, on looking at her, I observed her eyes fixed upon me. I wore a scarlet cloak trimmed with cock's feathers and a black, three-cornered hat. When we arrived at our station, the old lady tipped a porter to find out from my luggage who I was; and when she died—several years later—she left me in her will one of my most valuable jewels. This was Lady Margaret Beaumont; and I made both her acquaintance and friendship before her death.

Lady Tennyson was an invalid; and we were received on our arrival by the poet. Tennyson was a magnificent creature to look at. He had everything: height, figure, carriage, features and expression. Added to this he had what George Meredith said of him to me, "the feminine hint to perfection." He greeted me by saying:

"Well, are you as clever and spurty as your sister Laura?"

I had never heard the word "spurty" before, nor indeed have I since. To answer this kind of frontal attack one has to be either saucy or servile; so I said nothing memorable. We sat down to tea and he asked me if I wanted him to dress for dinner, adding:

"Your sister said of me, you know, that I was both untidy and dirty."

To which I replied:

"Did you mind this?"

TENNYSON: "I wondered if it was true. Do you think I'm dirty?"

MARGOT: "You are very handsome."

TENNYSON: "I can see by that remark that you think I am. Very well then, I will dress for dinner. Have you read Jane Welsh Carlyle's letters?"

MARGOT: "Yes, I have, and I think them excellent. It seems a pity," I added, with the commonplace that is apt to overcome one in a first conversation with a man of eminence, "that they were ever married; with any one but each other, they might have been perfectly happy."

TENNYSON: "I totally disagree with you. By any other arrangement four people would have been unhappy instead of two."

[48]

LADY DESBROUGH, WHOM MARGOT CALLS THE
CLEVEREST WOMAN IN ENGLAND

After this I went up to my room. The hours kept at Aldworth were peculiar; we dined early and after dinner the poet went to bed. At ten o'clock he came downstairs and, if asked, would read his poetry to the company till past midnight.

I dressed for dinner with great care that first night and, placing myself next to him when he came down, I asked him to read out loud to me.

TENNYSON: "What do you want me to read?"

MARGOT: "*Maud.*"

TENNYSON: "That was the poem I was cursed for writing! When it came out no word was bad enough for me! I was a blackguard, a ruffian and an atheist! You will live to have as great a contempt for literary critics and the public as I have, my child!"

While he was speaking, I found on the floor, among piles of books, a small copy of *Maud,* a shilling volume, bound in blue paper. I put it into his hands and, pulling the lamp nearer him, he began to read.

There is only one man—a poet also—who reads as my host did; and that is my beloved friend, Professor Gilbert Murray. When I first heard him at Oxford, I closed my eyes and felt as if the old poet were with me again.

Tennyson's reading had the lilt, the tenderness and the rhythm that makes music in the soul. It was neither singing, nor chanting, nor speaking, but a subtle mixture of the three; and the effect upon me was one of haunting harmonies that left me profoundly moved.

He began, " Birds in the high Hall-garden," and, skipping the next four sections, went on to, " I have led her home, my love, my only friend," and ended with:

> There has fallen a splendid tear
> From the passion-flower at the gate.
> She is coming, my dove, my dear,
> She is coming, my life, my fate;
> The red rose cries, "She is near, she is near;"
> And the white rose weeps, "She is late;"
> The larkspur listens, "I hear, I hear;"
> And the lily whispers, "I wait."
>
> She is coming, my own, my sweet;
> Were it ever so airy a tread,
> My heart would hear her and beat,
> Were it earth in an earthly bed;
> My dust would hear her and beat,
> Had I lain for a century dead;
> Would start and tremble under her feet,
> And blossom in purple and red.

Sir Walter.

O great & gallant Scot,
    True gentleman, heart blood & bone,
I would it had been my lot
    To have seen you, & heard you, & known!

Tennyson

Lord Tennyson wrote this for me: Aldworth 1884.

LORD TENNYSON'S TRIBUTE TO SIR WALTER SCOTT HITHERTO
UNPUBLISHED.

[51]

When he had finished, he pulled me on to his knee and said:

"Many may have written as well as that, but nothing that ever sounded so well!"

I could not speak.

He then told us that he had had an unfortunate experience with a young lady to whom he was reading *Maud*.

"She was sitting on my knee," he said, "as you are doing now, and after reading,

> Birds in the high Hall-garden
> When twilight was falling,
> Maud, Maud, Maud, Maud,
> They were crying and calling,

I asked her what bird she thought I meant. She said, 'A nightingale.' This made me so angry that I nearly flung her to the ground: 'No, fool! . . . Rook!' said I."

I got up, feeling rather sorry for the young lady, but was so afraid he was going to stop reading that I quickly opened *The Princess* and put it into his hands, and he went on.

I still possess the little *Maud,* bound in its blue paper cover, out of which he read to us, with my name written in it by Tennyson.

The morning after my arrival I was invited by our host to go for a walk with him, which flattered me very much; but after walking at a great pace over rough ground for two hours I regretted my vanity. Except my brother Glenconner I never met such an easy mover. The most characteristic feature left on my mind of that walk was Tennyson's appreciation of other poets.

. . . . . . .

Writing of poets, I come to George Wyndham.* It would be superfluous to add anything to what has already been published of him, but he was among the best-looking and most lovable of my circle.

He was a young man of nature endowed with even greater beauty than his sister, Lady Glenconner, but with less of her literary talent. Although his name will always be associated with the Irish Land Act, he was more interested in literature than politics, and, with a little self-discipline, might have been eminent in both.

Mr. Harry Cust is the last of the Souls that I intend writing about and was in some ways the rarest and the most brilliant of them all. Some one

*The late Right Hon. George Wyndham.

who knew him well wrote truly of him after he died:

"He tossed off the cup of life without fear of it containing any poison, but like many wilful men he was deficient in will-power."

The first time I ever saw Harry Cust was in Grosvenor Square, where he had come to see my sister Laura. A few weeks later I found her making a sachet, which was an unusual occupation for her, and she told me it was for "Mr. Cust," who was going to Australia for his health.

He remained abroad for over a year and, on the night of the Jubilee, 1887, he walked into our house where we were having supper. He had just returned from Australia, and was terribly upset to hear that Laura was dead.

Harry Cust had an untiring enthusiasm for life. At Eton he had been captain of the school and he was a scholar of Trinity. He had as fine a memory as Professor Churton Collins or my husband and an unplumbed sea of knowledge, quoting with equal ease both poetry and prose. He edited the *Pall Mall Gazette* brilliantly for several years. With his youth, brains and looks, he might have done anything in life; but he was fatally self-indulgent and success with my sex damaged his public career.

[55]

He was a fastidious critic and a faithful friend, fearless, reckless and unforgettable.

He wrote one poem, which appeared anonymously in the Oxford Book of English Verse:

Not unto us, O Lord,
Not unto us the rapture of the day,
The peace of night, or love's divine surprise,
High heart, high speech, high deeds 'mid honouring
 eyes;
For at Thy word
All these are taken away.

Not unto us, O Lord:
To us Thou givest the scorn, the scourge, the scar,
The ache of life, the loneliness of death,
The insufferable sufficiency of breath;
And with Thy sword
Thou piercest very far.

Not unto us, O Lord:
Nay, Lord, but unto her be all things given—
My light and life and earth and sky be blasted—
But let not all that wealth of love be wasted:
Let Hell afford
The pavement of her Heaven!

I print also a letter in verse sent to me on October 20th, 1887:

I came in to-night, made as woful as worry can,
Heart like a turnip and head like a hurricane,

[56]

# AN AUTOBIOGRAPHY

When lo! on my dull eyes there suddenly leaped a
Bright flash of your writing, du Herzensgeliebte;
And I found that the life I was thinking so leavable
Had still something in it made living conceivable;
And that, spite of the sores and the bores and the
    flaws in it,
My own life's the better for small bits of yours in it;
And it's only to tell you just that that I write to
    you,
And just for the pleasure of saying good night to
    you:
For I've nothing to tell you and nothing to talk
    about,
Save that I eat and I sleep and I walk about.
Since three days past does the indolent I bury
Myself in the British Museum Lib'ary,
Trying in writing to get in my hand a bit,
And reading Dutch books that I don't understand
    a bit:
But to-day Lady Charty and sweet Mrs. Lucy em-
Broidered the dusk of the British Museum,
And made me so happy by talking and laughing on
That I loved them more than the frieze of the
    Parthenon.
But I'm sleepy I know and don't know if I silly
    ain't;
Dined to-night with your sisters, where Tommy
    was brilliant;
And, while I the rest of the company deafened, I
Dallied awhile with your auntlet of seventy,
While one, Mr. Winsloe, a volume before him,
Regarded us all with a moody decorum.

No, I can't keep awake, and so, bowing and blessing
    you,
And seeing and loving (while slowly undressing)
    you,
Take your small hand and kiss, with a drowsed
    benediction, it
Knowing, as you, I'm your ever affectionate
                      HARRY C. C.

    .      .      .      .      .      .      .

I had another friend, James Kenneth Stephen, too pagan, wayward and lonely to be available for the Souls, but a man of genius. One afternoon he came to see me in Grosvenor Square and, being told by the footman that I was riding in the Row, he asked for tea and, while waiting for me wrote the following parody of Kipling and left it on my writing-table with his card:

P.S. THE MAN WHO WROTE IT.

---

We all called him The Man who Wrote It. And we called It what the man wrote, or *It* for short— all of us that is, except The Girl who Read It. She never called anything "It." She wasn't that sort of girl, but she read It, which was a pity from the point of view of The Man who Wrote It.

The man is dead now.

Dropped down a cud out beyond Karachi, and was brought home more like broken meat in a basket. But that's another story.

[58]

# AN AUTOBIOGRAPHY

The girl read It, and told It, and forgot all about It, and in a week It was all over the station. I heard it from Old Bill Buffles at the club while we were smoking between a peg and a hot weather dawn.

J. K. S.

I was delighted with this. Another time he wrote a parody of Myers' *St. Paul* for me. I will only quote one verse out of the eight:

Lo! what the deuce I'm always saying "Lo!" for
God is aware and leaves me uninformed.
Lo! there is nothing left for me to go for,
Lo! there is naught inadequately formed.

He ended by signing his name and writing:

Souvenez-vous si les vers que je trace
Fussent parfois (je l'avoue!) l'argot,
Si vous trouvez un peu trop d'audace
On ose tout quand on se dit
"Margot."

My dear friend J.K.S. was responsible for the aspiration frequently quoted:

When the Rudyards cease from Kipling
And the Haggards ride no more.

. . . . . .

Although I can hardly claim Symonds as a Soul, he was so much interested in me and my friends that I must write a short account of him.

I was nursing my sister, Pauline Gordon Duff, when I first met John Addington Symonds, in 1885, at Davos.

I climbed up to Am Hof* one afternoon with a letter of introduction, which was taken to the family while I was shown into a wooden room full of charming things. As no one came near me, I presumed every one was out, so I settled down peacefully among the books, prepared to wait. In a little time I heard a shuffle of slippered feet and some one pausing at the open door.

"Hass he gone?" was the querulous question that came from behind the screen.

And in a moment the thin, curious face of John Addington Symonds was peering at me round the corner.

There was nothing for it but to answer:

"No I am afraid she is still here!"

Being the most courteous of men, he smiled and took my hand; and we went up to his library together.

Symonds and I became very great friends.

After putting my sister to bed at 9.30, I climbed every night by starlight up to Am Hof, where we

*J. A. Symonds's country house.

talked and read out loud till one and often two in the morning. I learnt more in those winter nights at Davos than I had ever learnt in my life. We read *The Republic* and all the Plato dialogues together; Swift, Voltaire, Browning, Walt Whitman, Edgar Poe and Symonds' own *Renaissance,* besides passages from every author and poet, which he would turn up feverishly to illustrate what he wanted me to understand.

I shall always think Lord Morley* the best talker I ever heard and after him I would say Symonds, Birrell and Bergson. George Meredith was too much of a *prima donna* and was very deaf and uninterruptable when I knew him, but he was amazingly good even then. Alfred Austin was a friend of his and had just been made Poet Laureate by Lord Salisbury, when my beloved friend Admiral Maxse took me down to the country to see Meredith for the first time. Feeling more than usually stupid, I said to him:

"Well Mr. Meredith, I wonder what your friend Alfred Austin thinks of his appointment?"

Shaking his beautiful head he replied:

"It is very hard to say what a bantam is thinking when it is crowing."

*Viscount Morley of Blackburn.

Symonds' conversation is described in Stevenson's essay on *Talks and Talkers,* but no one could ever really give the fancy, the epigram, the swiftness and earnestness with which he not only expressed himself but engaged you in conversation. This and his affection combined to make him an enchanting companion.

The Swiss postmen and woodmen constantly joined us at midnight and drank Italian wines out of beautiful glass which our host had brought from Venice; and they were our only interruptions when Mrs. Symonds and the handsome girls went to bed. I have many memories of seeing our peasant friends off from Symonds' front door, and standing by his side in the dark, listening to the crack of their whips and their yodels yelled far down the snow roads into the starry skies.

When I first left him and returned to England, Mrs. Symonds told me he sat up all night, filling a blank book with his own poems and translations, which he posted to me in the early morning. We corresponded till he died; and I have kept every letter that he ever wrote to me.

He was the first person who besought me to write. If only he were alive now, I would show him this manuscript and, if any one could make any thing of it by counsel, sympathy and encouragement; my autobiography might become famous.

"You have *l'oreille juste,*" he would say, "and I value your literary judgment."

I will here insert some of his letters, beginning with the one he sent down to our villa at Davos *à propos* of the essays over which Lady Londonderry and I had our little breeze:

I am at work upon a volume of essays in art and criticism, puzzling to my brain and not easy to write. I think I shall ask you to read them.

I want an intelligent audience before I publish them. I want to "try them on" somebody's mind —like a dress—to see how they fit. Only you must promise to write observations and, most killing remark of all,, to say when the tedium of reading them begins to overweigh the profit of my philosophy.

I think you could help me.

After the publication he wrote:

I am sorry that the Essays I dedicated to you have been a failure—as I think they have been— to judge by the opinions of the Press. I wanted, when I wrote them, only to say the simple truth of what I thought and felt in the very simplest language I could find.

What the critics say is that I have uttered truisms in the baldest, least attractive diction.

Here I find myself to be judged, and not unjustly. In the pursuit of truth, I said what I had to say bluntly—and it seems I had nothing but commonplaces to give forth. In the search for sincerity of style, I reduced every proposition to its barest form of language. And that abnegation of rhetoric has revealed the nudity of my commonplaces.

I know that I have no wand, that I cannot conjure, that I cannot draw the ears of men to listen to my words.

So, when I finally withdraw from further appeals to the public, as I mean to do, I cannot pose as a Prospero who breaks his staff. I am only a somewhat sturdy, highly nervous varlet in the sphere of art, who has sought to wear the robe of the magician—and being now disrobed, takes his place quietly where God appointed him, and means to hold his tongue in future, since his proper function has been shown him.

Thus it is with me. And I should not, my dear friend, have inflicted so much of myself upon you, if I had not, unluckily, and in gross miscalculation of my powers, connected your name with the book which proves my incompetence.

Yes, the Master* is right: make as much of your life as you can: use it to the best and noblest purpose: do not, when you are old and broken like me, sit in the middle of the ruins of Carthage you have vainly conquered, as I am doing now.

*Dr. Jowett, Master of Balliol.

GODFREY WEBB: MEMBER OF THE SOULS AND GODFATHER
OF PRINCESS BIBESCO

Now good bye. Keep any of my letters which seem to you worth keeping. This will make me write better. I keep a great many of yours. You will never lose a warm corner in the centre of the heart of your friend

J. A. SYMONDS.

**P.S.** Live well. Live happy. Do not forget me. I like to think of you in plenitude of life and activity. I should not be sorry for you if you broke your neck in the hunting field. But, like the Master, I want you to make sure of the young, powerful life you have—before the inevitable, dolorous, long, dark night draws nigh.

Later on, à *propos* of his translation of the Autobiography of Benvenuto Cellini, he wrote:

I am so glad that you like my Cellini. The book has been a success; and I am pleased, though I am not interested in its sale. The publisher paid me £210 for my work, which I thought very good wages.

MY DEAR MARGOT,
I wrote to you in a great hurry yesterday, and with some bothering thoughts in the background of my head.

So I did not tell you how much I appreciated your critical insight into the points of my Introduction to Cellini. I do not rate that piece of writing quite as highly as you do. But you "spotted" the best thing in it—the syllogism describing Cellini's state of mind as to Bourbon's death.

[65]

It is true, I think, what you say: that I have been getting more nervous and less elaborate in style of late years. This is very natural. One starts in life with sensuous susceptibilities to beauty, with a strong feeling for colour and for melodious cadence, and also with an impulsive enthusiastic way of expressing oneself. This causes young work to seem decorated and laboured, whereas it very often is really spontaneous and hasty, more instructive and straightforward than the work of middle life. I write now with much more trouble and more slowly, and with much less interest in my subject than I used to do. This gives me more command over the vehicle, language, than I used to have. I write what pleases myself less, but what probably strikes other people more.

This is a long discourse; but not so much about myself as appears. I was struck with your insight, and I wanted to tell you how I analyse the change of style which you point out, and which results, I think, from colder, more laborious, duller effort as one grows in years.

The artist ought never to be commanded by his subject, or his vehicle of expression. But until he ceases to love both with a blind passion, he will probably be so commanded. And then his style will appear decorative, florid, mixed, unequal, laboured. It is the sobriety of a satiated or blunted enthusiasm which makes the literary artist. He ought to remember his dithyrambic moods, but not to be subject to them any longer, nor to yearn after them.

Do you know that I have only just now found

the time, during my long days and nights in bed with influenza and bronchitis, to read Marie Bashkirtseff? (Did ever name so puzzling grow upon the Ygdrasil of even Russian life?)

By this time you must be quite tired of hearing from your friends how much Marie Bashkirtseff reminds them of you.

I cannot help it. I must say it once again. I am such a fossil that I permit myself the most antediluvian remarks—if I think they have a grain of truth in them. Of course, the dissimilarities are quite as striking as the likenesses. No two leaves on one linden are really the same. But you and she, detached from the forest of life, seem to me like leaves plucked from the same sort of tree.

It is a very wonderful book. If only *messieurs les romanciers* could photograph experience in their fiction as she has done in some of her pages! The episode of Pachay, short as that is, is masterly— above the reach of Balzac; how far above the laborious, beetle-flight of Henry James! Above even George Meredith. It is what James would give his right hand to do once. The episode of Antonelli is very good, too, but not so exquisite as the other.

There is something pathetic about both "Asolando" and "Demeter," those shrivelled blossoms from the stout old laurels touched with frost of winter and old age. But I find little to dwell upon in either of them. Browning has more sap of life— Tennyson more ripe and mellow mastery. Each is here in the main reproducing his mannerism.

I am writing to you, you see, just as if I had not

been silent for so long. I take you at your word, and expect Margot to be always the same to a comrade.

If you were only here! Keats said that "heard melodies are sweet, but those unheard are sweeter." How false!

> Yes, thus it is: somewhere by me
> Unheard, by me unfelt, unknown,
> The laughing, rippling notes of thee
> Are sounding still; while I alone
> Am left to sit and sigh and say—
> Music unheard is sweet as they.

This is no momentary mood, and no light bubble-breath of improvisatory verse. It expresses what I often feel when, after a long night's work, I light my candle and take a look before I go to bed at your portrait in the corner of my stove.

I have been labouring intensely at my autobiography. It is blocked out, and certain parts of it are written for good. But a thing of this sort ought to be a master's final piece of work—and it is very exhausting to produce.

AM HOF,
DAVOS PLATZ,
SWITZERLAND,
*Sept. 27th,* 1891.

MY DEAR MARGOT,

I am sending you back your two typewritten records. They are both very interesting, the one as autobiographical and a study of your family, the other as a vivid and, I think, justly critical picture of Gladstone. It will have a great literary value sometime. I do not quite feel with Jowett, who told you, did he not? that you had made him *understand* Gladstone. But I feel that you have offered an extremely powerful and brilliant conception, which is impressive and convincing because of your obvious sincerity and breadth of view. The purely biographical and literary value of this bit of work seems to me very great, and makes me keenly wish that you would record all your interesting experiences, and your first-hand studies of exceptional personalities in the same way.

Gradually, by doing this, you would accumulate material of real importance; much better than novels or stories, and more valuable than the passionate utterances of personal emotion.

Did I ever show you the record I privately printed of an evening passed by me at Woolner, the sculptor's, when Gladstone met Tennyson for the first time? If I had been able to enjoy more of such incidents, I should also have made documents. But my opportunities have been limited. For future historians, the illuminative value of such writing will be incomparable.

I suppose I must send the two pieces back to Glen. Which I will do, together with this letter. Let me see what you write. I think you have a very penetrative glimpse into character, which comes from perfect disengagement and sympathy controlled by a critical sense. The absence of egotism is a great point.

. . . . . . .

# MARGOT ASQUITH

When Symonds died I lost my best intellectual tutor as well as one of my dearest friends. I wish I had taken his advice and seriously tried to write years ago, but, except for a few magazine sketches, I have never written a line for publication in my life. I have only kept a careful and accurate diary,* and here, in the interests of my publishers and at the risk of being thought egotistical, it is not inappropriate that I should publish the following letters in connection with these diaries and my writing:

21 CARLYLE MANSIONS,
CHEYNE WALK,
S. W.
*April 9th,* 1915.

MY DEAR MARGOT ASQUITH,

By what felicity of divination were you inspired to send me a few days ago that wonderful diary under its lock and key?—feeling so rightly certain, I mean, of the peculiar degree and particular *pang* of interest that I should find in it? I don't wonder, indeed, at your general presumption to that effect, but the mood, the moment, and the resolution itself conspired together for me, and I have absorbed every word of every page with the liveliest appreciation, and I think I may say intelligence. I have read the thing intimately, and I take off my hat to you as to the very Balzac of diarists. It is full of

---

*Out of all my diaries I have hardly been able to quote fifty pages, for on re-reading them I find they are not only full of Cabinet secrets but jerky, disjointed and dangerously frank.

[70]

life and force and colour, of a remarkable instinct
for getting close to your people and things and for
squeezing, in the case of the resolute portraits of
certain of your eminent characters, especially the
last drop of truth and sense out of them—at least
as the originals affected *your* singularly searching
vision. Happy, then, those who had, of this essence,
the fewest secrets or crooked lives to yield up to
you—for the more complicated and unimaginable
some of them appear, the more you seem to me to
have caught and mastered them. Then I have
found myself hanging on your impression in each
case with the liveliest suspense and wonder, so
thrillingly does the expression keep abreast of it
and really translate it. This and your extraordinary
fullness of opportunity, make of the record a most
valuable English document, a rare revelation of the
human inwardness of political life in this country,
and a picture of manners and personal characters
as "creditable" on the whole (to the country) as it
is frank and acute. The beauty is that you write
with such authority, that you've seen so much and
lived and moved so much, and that having so the
chance to observe and feel and discriminate in the
light of so much high pressure, you haven't been
in the least afraid, but have faced and assimilated
and represented for all you're worth.

I have lived, you see, wholly out of the inner
circle of political life, and yet more or less in won-
dering sight, for years, of many of its outer appear-
ances, and in superficial contact—though this,
indeed, pretty anciently now—with various actors
and figures, standing off from them on my quite

different ground and neither able nor wanting to be of the craft of mystery (preferring, so to speak, my own poor, private ones, such as they have been) and yet with all sorts of unsatisfied curiosities and yearnings and imaginings in your general, your fearful direction. Well, you take me by the hand and lead me back and in, and still in, and make things beautifully up to me—*all* my losses and misses and exclusions and privation—and do it by having taken all the right notes, apprehended all the right values and enjoyed all the right reactions— meaning by the right ones, those that must have ministered most to interest and emotion; those that I dimly made you out as getting while I flattened my nose against the shop window and you were there within, eating the tarts, shall I say, or handing them over the counter? It's to-day as if you had taken all the trouble for me and left me at last all the unearned increment or fine psychological gain! I have hovered about two or three of your distinguished persons a bit longingly (in the past) ; but you open up the abysses, or such like, that I really missed, and the torch you play over them is often luridly illuminating. I find my experience, therefore, the experience of simply reading you (you having had all t'other) veritably romantic. But I want so to go on that I deplore your apparent arrest—Saint Simon is in forty volumes—why should Margot be put in one? Your own portrait is an extraordinarily patient and detached and touch-upon-touch thing; but the book itself really constitutes an image of you by its strength of feeling and living individual tone. An admirable portrait of a lady, with no end of finish and style, is thereby projected, and if I don't stop now, I shall be calling it a regular masterpiece. Please believe how truly touched I am by your confidence in your faithful, though old, friend,

HENRY JAMES.

My dear and distinguished friend Lord Morley sent me the following letter of the 15th of September, 1919, and it was in consequence of this letter that, two months afterwards, on November the 11th, 1919, I began to write this book:

> FLOWERMEAD,
> PRINCES ROAD,
> WIMBLEDON PARK, S.W.,
> *September 15th,* 1919.

DEAR MRS. ASQUITH,

Your kindest of letters gave me uncommon pleasure, both personal and literary. Personal, because I like to know that we are still affectionate friends, as we have been for such long, important and trying years. Literary—because it is a brilliant example of that character-writing in which the French so indisputably beat us. If you like, you can be as keen and brilliant and penetrating as Madame de Sévigné or the best of them, and if I were a publisher, I would tempt you by high emoluments and certainty of fame. You ask me to leave you a book when I depart this life. If I were your generous well-wisher, I should not leave, but give you, my rather full collection of French Memoirs now while I am alive. Well, I am in very truth your best well-wisher, but incline to bequeath my modern library to a public body of female ladies, if you pardon that odd and inelegant expression.

I have nothing good or interesting to tell you of myself. My strength will stand no tax upon it.

The bequest from my old friend* in America was a pleasant refresher, and it touched me, considering how different we were in training, character, tastes, temperament. I was first introduced to him with commendation by Mr. Arnold—a curious trio, wasn't it? He thought, and was proud of it, that he, A. C., introduced M. A. and me to the United States.

I watch events and men here pretty vigilantly, with what good and hopeful spirits you can imagine. When you return do pay me a visit. There's nobody who would be such a tonic to an octogenarian.

Always, always, your affectionate friend,

J. M.

When I had been wrestling with this autobiography for two months I wrote and told John Morley of my venture, and this is his reply:

FLOWERMEAD,
PRINCES ROAD,
WIMBLEDON PARK,
S.W.,
(*Jan., 1920*).

DEAR MRS. ASQUITH,

A bird in the air had already whispered the

*Andrew Carnegie.

[74]

matter of your literary venture, and I neither had nor have any doubt at all that the publisher knew very well what he was about. The book will be bright in real knowledge of the world; rich in points of life; sympathetic with human nature, which in strength and weakness is never petty or small.

Be sure to *trust yourself;* and don't worry about critics. You need no words to tell you how warmly I am interested in your great design. *Persevere.*

How kind to bid me to your royal* meal. But I am too old for company that would be so new, so don't take it amiss, my best of friends, if I ask to be bidden when I should see more of *you.* You don't know how dull a man, once lively, can degenerate into being.

Your always affectionate and grateful

J. MORLEY.

.   .   .   .   .   .   .

To return to my triumphant youth: I will end this chapter with a note which my friend, Lady Frances Balfour—one of the few women of outstanding intellect that I have known—sent me from her father, the late Duke of Argyll, the wonderful orator of whom it was said that he was like a cannon being fired off by a canary.

Frances asked me to meet him at a small dinner and placed me next to him. In the course of our

*I invited him to meet the Prince of Wales.

conversation, he quoted these words that he had heard in a sermon preached by Dr. Caird:

"Oh! for the time when Church and State shall no longer be the watchword of opposing hosts, when every man shall be a priest and every priest shall be a king, as priest clothed with righteousness, as king with power!"

I made him write them down for me, and we discussed religion, preachers and politics at some length before I went home.

The next morning he wrote to his daughter:

ARGYLL LODGE,
KENSINGTON.

DEAR FRANCES,

How dare you ask me to meet a *syren*.

Your affectionate,

A.

# CHAPTER II

I SHALL open this chapter of my autobiography with a character-sketch of myself, written at Glen in one of our pencil-games in January, 1888. Nearly every one in the room guessed that I was the subject, but opinions differed as to the authorship. Some thought that our dear and clever friend, Godfrey Webb, had written it as a sort of joke.

"In appearance she was small, with rapid, nervous movements; energetic, never wholly ungraceful, but inclined to be restless. Her face did not betray the intelligence she possessed, as her eyes, though clear and well-shaped, were too close together. Her hawky nose was bent over a short upper lip and meaningless mouth. The chin showed more definite character than her other features, being large, bony and prominent, and she had curly, pretty hair, growing well on a finely-cut forehead; the *ensemble* healthy and mobile; in manner easy, unself-conscious, emphatic, inclined to be noisy from over-keenness and perfectly self-possessed. Conversation graphic and exaggerated, eager and concentrated, with a natural gift of expression. Her honesty more a peculiarity than a virtue. Decision more of instinct than of reason; a disengaged mind wholly unfettered by prejudice. Very observant and a fine judge of her fellow-creatures, finding all interesting and worthy of her speculation. She was not easily depressed by antagonistic circumstances or social situations hostile to herself—on the contrary, her spirit rose in all losing games. She was assisted in this by having no personal vanity, the highest vitality and great self-confidence. She was self-indulgent, though not selfish, and had not enough self-control for her passion and impetuosity; it was owing more to dash and grit than to any foresight that she kept out of difficulties. She distrusted the dried-up advice of many people, who prefer coining evil to publishing good. She was lacking in awe, and no respecter of persons; loving old people because she never felt they were old. Warm-hearted, and with much power of devotion, thinking no trouble too great to take for those you love, and agreeing with Dr. Johnson that friendships should be kept in constant repair. Too many interests and too many-sided. Fond of people, animals, books, sport, music, art and exercise. More Bohemian than exclusive and with a certain power of investing acquaintances and even bores with interest. Passionate love of Nature. Lacking in devotional, practising religion; otherwise sensitively religious. Sensible; not easily influenced for good or evil. Jealous, keen and faithful in affection. Great want of plodding perseverance, doing many things with promise and nothing well. A fine ear for music: no execution; a good eye for drawing: no knowledge or practice in perspective; more critical than constructive. Very cool and decided with horses. Good nerve, good whip and a fine rider. Intellectually self-made, ambitious, independent and self-willed. Fond of admiration and love from both men and women, and able to give it."

I sent this to Dr. Jowett with another character-sketch of Gladstone. After reading them, he wrote me this letter:

BALL. COLL.
*Oct.* 23rd, 1890.

MY DEAR MARGOT,

I return the book* which you entrusted to me: I was very much interested by it. The sketch of Gladstone is excellent. Pray write some more of it some time: I understand him better after reading it.

The young lady's portrait of herself is quite truthful and not at all flattered: shall I add a trait or two? "She is very sincere and extremely clever; indeed, her cleverness almost amounts to genius. She might be a distinguished authoress if she would —but she wastes her time and her gifts scampering about the world and going from one country house to another in a manner not pleasant to look back upon and still less pleasant to think of twenty years hence, when youth will have made itself wings and fled away."

If you know her, will you tell her with my love, that I do not like to offer her any more advice, but I wish that she would take counsel with herself. She has made a great position, though slippery and dangerous: will she not add to this a noble and simple life which can alone give a true value to it? The higher we rise, the more self-discipline, self-control and economy is required of us. It is a hard thing to be in the world but not of it; to be outwardly much like other people and yet to be cher-

*A commonplace book with a few written sketches of people in it.

ishing an ideal which extends over the whole of life and beyond; to have a natural love for every one, especially for the poor; to get rid, not of wit or good humour, but of frivolity and excitement; to live "selfless" according to the Will of God and not after the fashions and opinions of men and women.

Stimulated by this and the encouragement of Lionel Tennyson—a new friend—I was anxious to start a newspaper. When I was a little girl at Glen, there had been a schoolroom paper, called *"The Glen Gossip: The Tennant Tatler, or The Peeblesshire Prattler."* I believe my brother Eddy wrote the wittiest verses in it; but I was too young to remember much about it or to contribute anything. I had many distinguished friends by that time, all of whom had promised to write for me. The idea was four or five numbers to be illustrated by my sister Lucy Graham Smith, and a brilliant letter-press, but, in spite of much discussion among ourselves, it came to nothing. I have always regretted this, as, looking at the names of the contributors and the programme for the first number, I think it might have been a success. The title of the paper gave us infinite trouble. We ended by adopting a suggestion of my own, and our new venture was to have been called *"To-morrow."* This is the

list of people who promised to write for me, and the
names they suggested for the paper:

| | |
|---|---|
| Lord and Lady Pembroke | *Sympathetic Ink.* |
| | *The Idle Pen.* |
| | *The Mail.* |
| | *The Kite.* |
| | *Blue Ink.* |
| **Mr. A. Lyttelton** - - | *The Hen.* |
| | *The Cluck.* |
| Mr. Knowles - - - | *The Butterfly.* |
| **Mr. A. J. Balfour** - - | *The New Eve.* |
| | *Anonymous.* |
| | *Mrs. Grundy.* |
| **Mr. Oscar Wilde** - - | *The Life Improver.* |
| | *Mrs. Grundy's Daughter.* |
| Lady Ribblesdale - - | *Jane.* |
| | *Psyche.* |
| | *The Mask.* |
| Margot Tennant - - | *The Mangle.* |
| | *Eve.* |
| | *Dolly Varden.* |
| | *To-morrow.* |
| Mr. Webb - - - | *The Petticoat.* |
| Mrs. Horner - - - | *She.* |
| Miss Mary Leslie - - | *The Sphinx.* |
| | *Eglantine.* |
| | *Blue Veil.* |
| | *Pinafore.* |
| Sir A. West - - - | *The Spinnet.* |
| | *The Spinning-Wheel.* |
| Mr. J. A. Symonds - - | *Muses and Graces.* |
| | *Causeries en peignoir.* |
| | *Woman's Wit and Humour.* |

The contributors on our staff were to have been
Laurence Oliphant, J. K. Stephen, Mr. Wilfrid

# AN AUTOBIOGRAPHY

Blunt, Hon. George Curzon, George Wyndham, Godfrey Webb, Doll Liddell, Harry Cust, Mr. Knowles (the editor of the *Nineteenth Century*), the Hon. A. Lyttelton, Mr. A. J. Balfour, Oscar Wilde, Lord and Lady Ribblesdale, Mrs. (now Lady) Horner, Sir Algernon West, Lady Frances Balfour, Lord and Lady Pembroke, Miss Betty Ponsonby (the present Mrs. Montgomery), John Addington Symonds, Dr. Jowett (the Master of Balliol), M. Coquelin, Sir Henry Irving, Miss Ellen Terry, Sir Edward Burne-Jones, Mr. George Russell, Mrs. Singleton (alias Violet Fane, afterwards Lady Currie), Lady de Grey, Lady Constance Leslie and the Hon. Lionel Tennyson.

Our programme for the first number was to have been the following:

### TO-MORROW

| | | |
|---|---|---|
| *Leader* | Persons and Politics | Margot Tennant. |
| *The Social Zodiac* | Rise and fall of Professional Beauties | Lady de Grey. |
| *Occasional Articles* | The Green-eyed Monster | Violet Fane (*nom-de-plume* of Mrs. Singleton). |
| *Occasional Notes* | Foreign and Colonial Gossip | Harry Cust. |
| *Men and Women* | Character Sketch | Margot Tennant. |
| *Story* - - - | - - - - - - | Oscar Wilde. |
| *Poem* - - - | - - - - - | Godfrey Webb. |
| *Letters to Men* - | - - - - - | George Wyndham. |
| *Books Reviewed* - | - - - - - | John Addington Symonds. |
| *Conversations* - | - - - - - - | Miss Ponsonby. |

This is what I wrote for the first number:

"PERSONS AND POLITICS

"In Politics the common opinion is that measures are the important thing, and that men are merely the instruments which each generation produces, equal or unequal to the accomplishment of them.

"This is a mistake. The majority of mankind desire nothing so much as to be led. They have no opinions of their own, and, half from caution, half from laziness, are willing to leave the responsibility to any stronger person. It is the personality of the man which makes the masses turn to him, gives influence to his ideas while he lives, and causes him to be remembered after both he and his work are dead. From the time of Moses downwards, history abounds in such examples. In the present century Napoleon and Gladstone have perhaps impressed themselves most dramatically on the public mind, and, in a lesser degree, Disraeli and Parnell. The greatest men in the past have been superior to their age and associated themselves with its glory only in so far as they have contributed to it. But in these days the movement of time is too rapid for us to recognise such a man: under modern conditions he

[84]

must be superior, not so much to his age, as to the men of his age, and absorb what glory he can in his own personality.

"The Code Napoléon remains, but, beyond this, hardly one of Napoleon's great achievements survives as a living embodiment of his genius. Never was so vast a fabric so quickly created and so quickly dissolved. The moment the individual was caught and removed, the bewitched French world returned to itself; and the fame of the army and the *prestige* of France were as mere echoes of retreating thunder. Dead as are the results of Bonaparte's measures and actions, no one would question the permanent vitality of his name. It conjures up an image in the dullest brain; and among all historical celebrities he is the one whom most of us would like to have met.

"The Home Rule question, which has long distorted the public judgment and looms large at the present political moment, admirably illustrates the power of personality. Its importance has been exaggerated; the grant of Home Rule will not save Ireland; its refusal will not shame England. Its swollen proportions are wholly due to the passionate personal feelings which Mr. Gladstone alone among living statemen inspires. 'He is so powerful that his thoughts are nearly acts,' as some one has written of him; and at an age when most men would be wheeled into the chimney-corner, he is at the head of a precarious majority and still retains enough force to compel its undivided support.

"Mr. Chamberlain's power springs from the concentration of a nature which is singularly free from complexity. The range of his mind is narrow, but up to its horizon the whole is illuminated by the same strong and rather garish light. The absoluteness of his convictions is never shaded or softened by any play of imagination or sympathetic insight. It is not in virtue of any exceptionally fine or attractive quality, either of intellect or of character, that Mr. Chamberlain has become a dominant figure. Strength of will, directness of purpose, an aggressive and contagious belief in himself: these—which are the notes of a compelling individuality—made him what he is. On the other hand, culture, intellectual versatility, sound and practised judgment, which was tried and rarely found wanting in delicate and even dangerous situations, did not suffice in the case of Mr. Matthews to redeem the shortcomings of a diffuse and ineffective personality.

"In a different way, Mr. Goschen's remarkable endowments are neutralised by the same limitations. He has infinite ingenuity, but he can neither initiate nor propel; an intrepid debater in council and in action, he is prey to an invincible indecision.

"If the fortunes of a Government depend not so much on its measures as upon the character of the men who compose it, the new Ministry starts with every chance of success.

"Lord Rosebery is one of our few statesmen whose individuality is distinctly recognised by the public, both at home and abroad.

"Lord Spencer, without a trace of genius, is a person. Sir W. Harcourt, the most brilliant and witty of them all, is, perhaps, not more than a lifelike imitation of a strong man. Mr. John Morley has conviction, courage and tenacity; but an overdelicacy of nervous organisation and a certain lack of animal spirits disqualify him from being a leader of men.

"It is premature to criticise the new members of the Cabinet, of whom the most conspicuous is Mr. Asquith. Beyond and above his abilities and eloquence, there is in him much quiet force and a certain vein of scornful austerity. His supreme contempt for the superficial and his independence of mind might take him far.

"The future will not disclose its secrets, but personality still governs the world, and the avenue is open to the man, wherever he may be found, who can control and will not be controlled by fashions of opinion and the shifting movement of causes and cries."

My article is not at all good, but I put it in this autobiography merely as a political prophecy.

.      .      .      .      .      .      .

To be imitative and uninfluenceable—although a common combination—is a bad one. I am not tempted to be imitative except, I hope, in the better sense of the word, but I regret to own that I am not very influenceable either.

Jowett (the Master of Balliol in 1888-89), my doctor, Sir John Williams (of Aberystwyth), my son Anthony and old Lady Wemyss (the mother of the present Earl) had more influence over me than any other individuals in the world.

The late Countess of Wemyss, who died in 1896,

was a great character without being a character-part. She told me that she frightened people, which distressed her. As I am not easily frightened, I was puzzled by this. After thinking it over, I was convinced that it was because she had a hard nut to crack within herself: she possessed a jealous, passionate, youthful temperament, a formidable standard of right and wrong, a distinguished and rather stern *accueil,* a low, slow utterance and terrifying sincerity. She was the kind of person I had dreamt of meeting and never knew that God had made. She once told me that I was the best friend man, woman or child could ever have. After this wonderful compliment, we formed a deep attachment, which lasted until her death. She had a unique power of devotion and fundamental humbleness. I kept every letter she ever wrote to me.

When we left Downing Street in ten days—after being there for over nine years—and had not a roof to cover our heads, our new friends came to the rescue. I must add that many of the old ones had no room for us and some were living in the country. Lady Crewe*—young enough to be my daughter, and a woman of rare honesty of purpose and clear-

*The Marchioness of Crewe.

ness of head—took our son Cyril in at Crewe House. Lady Granard* put up my husband; Mrs. Cavendish-Bentinck—Lady Granard's aunt and one of God's own—befriended my daughter Elizabeth; Mrs. George Keppel†always large-hearted and kind—gave me a whole floor of her house in Grosvenor Street to live in, for as many months as I liked, and Mrs. McKenna‡ took in my son Anthony. No one has had such wonderful friends as I have had, but no one has suffered more at discovering the instability of human beings and how little power to love many people possess.

Few men and women surrender their wills; and it is considered lowering to their dignity to own that they are in the wrong. I never get over my amazement at this kind of self-value, it passes all my comprehension. It is vanity and this fundamental lack of humbleness that is the bed-rock of nearly every quarrel.

It was through my beloved Lady Wemyss that I first met the Master of Balliol. One evening in 1888, after the men had come in from shooting, we

*The Countess of Granard.
†The Hon. Mrs. Keppel.
‡Mrs. McKenna, the daughter of Lady Jekyll, and niece of Lady Horner.

were having tea in the large marble hall at Gosford.*  I generally wore an accordion skirt at tea, as Lord Wemyss liked me to dance to him.  Some one was playing the piano and I was improvising in and out of the chairs, when, in the act of making a final curtsey, I caught my foot in my skirt and fell at the feet of an old clergyman seated in the window.  As I got up, a loud "Damn!" resounded through the room.  Recovering my presence of mind, I said, looking up:

"You are a clergyman and I am afraid I have shocked you!"

"Not at all," he replied.  "I hope you will go on; I like your dancing extremely."

I provoked much amusement by asking the family afterwards if the parson whose presence I had failed to notice was their minister at Aberlady. I then learnt that he was the famous Dr. Benjamin Jowett, Master of Balliol.

Before telling how my friendship with the Master developed, I shall go back to the events in Oxford which gave him his insight into human beings and caused him much quiet suffering.

*Gosford is the Earl of Wemyss' country place and is situated between Edinburgh and North Berwick.

In 1852 the death of Dr. Jenkyns caused the Mastership at Balliol to become vacant. Jowett's fame as a tutor was great, but with it there had spread a suspicion of "rationalism." Persons whispered that the great tutor was tainted with German views. This reacted unduly upon his colleagues; and, when the election came, he was rejected by a single vote. His disappointment was deep, but he threw himself more than ever into his work. He told me that a favourite passage of his in Marcus Aurelius—"Be always doing something serviceable to mankind and let this constant generosity be your only pleasure, not forgetting a due regard to God"—had been of great help to him at that time.

The lectures which his pupils cared most about were those on Plato and St. Paul; both as tutor and examiner he may be said to have stimulated the study of Plato in Oxford: he made it a rival to that of Aristotle.

"Aristotle is dead," he would say, "but Plato is alive."

Hitherto he had published little—an anonymous essay on Pascal and a few literary articles—but under the stimulus of disappointment he finished his share of the edition of St. Paul's Epistles, which had been undertaken in conjunction with Arthur Stanley. Both produced their books in 1855; but while Stanley's *Corinthians* evoked languid interest, Jowett's *Galatians, Thessalonians* and *Romans* provoked a clamour among his friends and enemies. About that time he was appointed to the Oxford Greek Chair, which pleased him much; but his delight was rather dashed by a hostile article in the *Quarterly Review,* abusing him and his religious writings. The Vice-Chancellor, Dr. Cotton, required from him a fresh signature of the Articles of the Church of England. At the interview, when addressed by two men—one pompously explaining that it was a necessary act if he was to retain his cloth and the other apologising for inflicting a humiliation upon him—he merely said:

"Give me the pen."

His essay on *The Interpretation of Scripture,* which came out in 1860 in the famous volume, *Essays and Reviews,* increased the cry of heterodoxy against him; and the Canons of Christ Church, including Dr. Pusey, persisted in withholding from him an extra salary, without which the endowment of the Greek Chair was worth £40. This scandal was not removed till 1864, after he had been excluded from the university pulpit. He continued working hard at his translation of the whole of Plato; he had already published notes on the *Republic* and analyses of the dialogue. This took up all his time till 1878, when he became Master of Balliol.

The worst of the *Essays and Reviews* controversy was that it did an injustice to Jowett's reputation. For years people thought that he was a great heresiarch presiding over a college of infidels and heretics. His impeached article on *The Interpretation of Scripture* might to-day be published by any clergyman. His crime lay in saying that the Bible should be criticised like other books.

In his introduction to the *Republic* of Plato he expresses the same thought:

A Greek in the age of Plato attached no importance to the question whether his religion was an historical fact. . . . Men only began to suspect that the narratives of Homer and Hesiod were fictions when they recognised them to be immoral. And so in all religions: the consideration of their morality comes first, afterwards the truth of the documents in which they are recorded, or of the events, natural or supernatural, which are told of them. But in modern times, and in Protestant countries perhaps more than Catholic, we have been too much inclined to identify the historical with the moral; and some have refused to believe in religion at all, unless a superhuman accuracy was discerned in every part of the record. The facts of an ancient or religious history are amongst the most important of all facts, but they are frequently uncertain, and we only learn the true lesson which is to be gathered from them when we place ourselves above them.

Some one writes in the Literary Supplement of the *Times* to-day, 11th December, 1919:

"An almost animal indifference to mental refinement characterises our great public."

This is quite true, and presumably was true in Jowett's day, not only of the great public but of the Established Church.

Catherine Marsh, the author of *The Life of Hedley Vicars,* wrote to Jowett assuring him of her complete belief in the sincerity of his religious views and expressing indignation that he should have had to sign the thirty-nine Articles again. I give his reply. The postscript is characteristic of his kindliness, gentle temper and practical wisdom.

*March* 16*th*, 1864.

DEAR MADAM,

Accept my best thanks for your kind letter, and for the books you have been so good as to send me.

[95]

I certainly hope (though conscious of how little I am able to do) that I shall devote my life to the service of God, and of the youths of Oxford, whom I desire to regard as a trust which He has given me. But I am afraid, if I may judge from the tenour of your letter, that I should not express myself altogether as you do on religious subjects. Perhaps the difference may be more than one of words. I will not, therefore, enter further into the grave question suggested by you, except to say that I am sure I shall be the better for your kind wishes and reading your books.

The recent matter of Oxford is of no real consequence, and is not worth speaking about, though I am very grately to you and others for feeling "indignant" at the refusal.

With sincere respect for your labours,

Believe me, dear Madam,

Most truly yours,

B. JOWETT.

P.S.—I have read your letter again! I think that I ought to tell you that, unless you had been a complete stranger, you would not have had so good an opinion of me. I feel the kindness of your letter, but at the same time, if I believed what you say of me, I should soon become a "very complete rascal." Any letter like yours, which is written with such earnestness, and in a time of illness, is a serious call to think about religion. I do not intend to neglect this because I am not inclined to use the same language.

[96]

EARL OF PEMBROKE: MEMBER OF THE SOULS

# AN AUTOBIOGRAPHY

When Jowett became Master, his pupils and friends gathered round him and overcame the Church chatter. He was the hardest-working tutor, Vice-Chancellor and Master that Oxford ever had. Balliol, under his *régime,* grew in numbers and produced more scholars, more thinkers and more political men of note than any other college in the university. He had authority and a unique *prestige.* It was said of Dr. Whewell of Trinity that "knowledge was his forte and omniscience his foible"; the same might have been said of the Master and was expressed in a college epigram, written by an undergraduate. After Jowett's death I cut the following from an Oxford magazine:

The author of a famous and often misquoted verse upon Professor Jowett has written me a note upon his lines which may be appropriately inserted here. "Several versions," he writes, "have appeared lately, and my vanity does not consider them improvements. The lines were written:

'First come I, my name is Jowett,
There's no knowledge but I know it.
I am Master of this College,
What I don't know—is not knowledge.'

"The 'First come I' referred to its being a masque of the College in which fellows, scholars, etc., appeared in order. The short, disconnected sentences were intentional, as being characteristic. Such a line as 'All that can be known I know it' (which some newspapers substituted for line 2) would express a rather vulgar, Whewellian foible of omniscience, which was quite foreign to the Master's nature; the line as originally written was intended to express the rather sad, brooding manner the Master had of giving his oracles, as though he were a spectator of all time and existence, and had penetrated into the mystery of things. Of course, the last line expressed, with necessary exaggeration, what, as a fact, was his attitude to certain subjects in which he refused to be interested, such as modern German metaphysics, philology, and Greek inscriptions."

When I met the Master in 1887, I was young and he was old; but, whether from insolence or insight, I never felt this difference. I do not think I was a good judge of age, as I have always liked older people than myself; and I imagine it was because of this unconsciousness that we became such wonderful friends. Jowett was younger than half the young people I know now and we understood each other perfectly. If I am hasty in making friends and skip the preface, I always read it afterwards.

A good deal of controversy has arisen over the

Master's claim to greatness by some of the younger generation. It is not denied that Jowett was a man of influence. Men as different as Huxley, Symonds, Lord Lansdowne, Lord Bowen, Lord Milner, Sir Robert Morier and others have told me in reverent and affectionate terms how much they owed to him and to his influence. It is not denied that he was a kind man; infinitely generous, considerate and good about money. It may be denied that he was a fine scholar of the first rank, such as Munro or Jebb, although no one denies his contributions to scholarship; but the real question remains: was he a great man? There are big men, men of intellect, intellectual men, men of talent and men of action; but the great man is difficult to find, and it needs— apart from discernment—a certain greatness to find him. The Almighty is a wonderful handicapper: He will not give us everything. I have never met a woman of supreme beauty with more than a mediocre intellect, by which I do not mean intelligence. There may be some, but I am only writing my own life, and I have not met them. A person of magnetism, temperament and quick intelligence may have neither intellect nor character. I have known one man whose genius lay in his rapid and sensitive understanding, real wit, amazing charm and apparent candour, but whose meanness, ingratitude and instability injured everything he touched. You can only discover ingratitude or instability after years of experience, and few of us, I am glad to think, ever suspect meanness in our fellow-creatures; the discovery is as painful when you find it as the discovery of a worm in the heart of a rose. A man may have a fine character and be taciturn, stubborn and stupid. Another may be brilliant, sunny and generous, but self-indulgent, heartless and a liar. There is no contradiction I have not met with in men and women: the rarest combination is to find fundamental humbleness, freedom from self, intrepid courage and the power to love; when you come upon these, you may be quite sure that you are in the presence of greatness.

Human beings are made up of a good many pieces. Nature, character, intellect and temperament: roughly speaking, these headings cover every one. The men and women whom I have loved best have been those whose natures were rich and sweet; but, alas, with a few exceptions, all of them have had gimcrack characters; and the qualities which I have loved in them have been ultimately submerged by self-indulgence.

The present Archbishop of Canterbury is one of these exceptions: he has a sweet and rich nature, a fine temper and is quite unspoilable. I have only one criticism to make of Randall Davidson: he has too much moderation for his intellect; but I daresay he would not have steered the Church through so many shallows if he had not had this attribute. I have known him since I was ten (he christened, confirmed, married and buried us all); and his faith in such qualities of head and heart as I possess has never wavered. He reminds me of Jowett in the soundness of his nature and his complete absence of vanity, although no two men were ever less alike. The first element of greatness is fundamental humbleness (this should not be confused with servility); the second is freedom from self; the third is intrepid courage, which, taken in its widest interpretation, generally goes with truth; and the fourth, the power to love, although I have put it last, is the rarest. If these go to the makings of a great man, Jowett possessed them all. He might have mocked at the confined comprehension of Oxford and exposed the arrogance, vanity and conventionality of the Church; intellectual scorn and even bitterness might have come to him; but, with infinite patience and imperturbable serenity, he preserved his faith in his fellow-creatures.

"There was in him a simple trust in the word of other men that won for him a devotion and service which discipline could never have evoked."*

Whether his criticisms of the Bible fluttered the faith of the flappers in Oxford, or whether his long silences made the undergraduates more stupid than they would otherwise have been, I care little: I only know that he was what I call great and that he had an ennobling influence over my life. He was apprehensive of my social reputation; and in our correspondence, which started directly we parted at Gosford, he constantly gave me wise advice. He was extremely simple-minded and had a pathetic belief in the fine manners, high tone, wide education and lofty example of the British aristocracy. It shocked him that I did not share it; I felt his warnings much as a duck swimming might feel the cluckings of a hen on the bank; nevertheless, I loved his exhortations. In one of his letters he begs me

---

*I read these words in an obituary notice the other day and thought how much I should like to have had them written of me.

to give up the idea of shooting bears with the Prince of Wales in Russia. It was the first I had heard of it! In another of his letters to me he ended thus:

But I must not bore you with good advice. Child, why don't you make a better use of your noble gifts? And yet you do not do anything wrong—only what other people do, but with more success. And you are very faithful to your friends. And so, God bless you.

He was much shocked by hearing that I smoked. This is what he says:

What are you doing—breaking a young man's heart; not the first time nor the second, nor the third —I believe? Poor fellows! they have paid you the highest compliment that a gentleman can pay a lady, and are deserving of all love. Shall I give you a small piece of counsel? It is better for you and a duty to them that their disappointed passions should never be known to a single person, for as you are well aware, one confidante means every body, and the good-natured world, who are of course very jealous of you, will call you cruel and a breaker of hearts, etc. I do not consider this advice, but merely a desire to make you see things as others see them or nearly. The Symonds girls at Davos told me that you smoked!!! at which I am shocked, because it is not the manner of ladies in England. I always imagine you with a long hookah puffing, puffing, since I heard this; give it up, my dear Margaret—it will get you a bad name.

Please do observe that I am always serious when I try to make fun. I hope you are enjoying life and friends and the weather: and believe me

Ever yours truly,

B. JOWETT.

He asked me once if I ever told any one that he wrote to me, to which I answered:

"I should rather think so! I tell every railway porter!"

This distressed him. I told him that he was evidently ashamed of my love for him, but that I was proud of it.

JOWETT (*after a long silence*): "Would you like to have your life written, Margaret?"

MARGOT: "Not much, unless it told the whole truth about me and every one and was indiscreet. If I could have a biographer like Froude or Lord Hervey, it would be divine, as no one would be bored by reading it. Who will you choose to write your life, Master?"

JOWETT: "No one will be in a position to write my life, Margaret." (For some time he called me Margaret; he thought it sounded less familiar than Margot.)

[104]

MARGOT: "What nonsense! How can you possibly prevent it? If you are not very good to me, I may even write it myself!"

JOWETT (*smiling*): "If I could have been sure of that, I need not have burnt all my correspondence! But you are an idle young lady and would certainly never have concentrated on so dull a subject."

MARGOT (*indignantly*): "Do you mean to say you have burnt all George Eliot's letters, Matthew Arnold's, Swinburne's, Temple's and Tennyson's?"

JOWETT: "I have kept one or two of George Eliot's and Florence Nightingale's; but great men do not write good letters."

MARGOT: "Do you know Florence Nightingale? I wish I did."

JOWETT (*evidently surprised that I had never heard the gossip connecting his name with Florence Nightingale*): "Why do you want to know her?"

MARGOT: "Because she was in love with my friend George Pembroke's* father."

JOWETT (*guardedly*): "Oh, indeed! I will take

*George, Earl of Pembroke, uncle of the present Earl.

you to see her and then you can ask her about all this."

MARGOT: "I should love that! But perhaps she would not care for me."

JOWETT: "I do not think she will care for you, but would you mind that?"

MARGOT: "Oh, not at all! I am quite unfeminine in those ways. When people leave the room, I don't say to myself, "I wonder if they like me," but, "I wonder if I like them.""

This made an impression on the Master, or I should not have remembered it. Some weeks after this he took me to see Florence Nightingale in her house in South Street. Groups of hospital nurses were waiting outside in the hall to see her. When we went in I noted her fine, handsome, well-bred face. She was lying on a sofa, with a white shawl round her shoulders and, after shaking hands with her, the Master and I sat down. She pointed to the beautiful Richmond print of Sidney Herbert, hanging above her mantelpiece, and said to me:

"I am interested to meet you, as I hear George Pembroke, the son of my old and dear friend, is devoted to you. Will you tell me what he is like?"

I described Lord Pembroke, while Jowett sat in stony silence till we left the house.

One day, a few months after this visit, I was driving in the vicinity of Oxford with the Master and I said to him:

"You never speak of your relations to me and you never tell me whether you were in love when you were young; I have told you so much about myself!"

JOWETT: "Have you ever heard that I was in love with any one?"

I did not like to tell him that, since our visit to Florence Nightingale, I had heard that he had wanted to marry her, so I said:

"Yes, I have been told you were in love once."

JOWETT: "Only once?"

MARGOT: "Yes."

Complete silence fell upon us after this: I broke it at last by saying:

"What was your lady-love like, dear Master?"

JOWETT: "Violent . . . very violent."

After this disconcerting description, we drove back to Balliol.

Mrs. Humphry Ward's novel *Robert Elsmere* had just been published and was dedicated to my sister Laura and Thomas Hill Green, Jowett's rival in Oxford. This is what the Master wrote to me about it:

*"Nov.* 28, 1888.

DEAR MISS TENNANT,

I have just finished examining for the Balliol Scholarships: a great institution of which you may possibly have heard. To what shall I liken it? It is not unlike a man casting into the sea a great dragnet, and when it is full of fish, pulling it up again and taking out fishes, good, bad and indifferent, and throwing the bad and indifferent back again into the sea. Among the good fish there have been Archbishop Tait, Dean Stanley, A. H. Clough, Mr. Arnold, Lord Coleridge, Lord Justice Bowen, Mr. Ilbert, &c., &c., &c. The institution was founded about sixty years ago.

I have been dining alone rather dismally, and now I shall imagine that I receive a visit from a young lady about twenty-three years of age, who enlivens me by her prattle. Is it her or her angel? But I believe that she is an angel, pale, volatile and like Laodamia in Wordsworth, ready to disappear at a moment's notice. I could write a description of her, but am not sure that I could do her justice.

I wish that I could say anything to comfort you, my dear Margot, or even to make you laugh. But no one can comfort another. The memory of a beautiful character is "a joy for ever," especially of one who was bound to you in ties of perfect amity. I saw what your sister* was from two

*Mrs. Gordon Duff.

short conversations which I had with her, and from the manner in which she was spoken of at Davos.

I send you the book* which I spoke of, though I hardly know whether it is an appropriate present; at any rate I do not expect you to read it. It has taken me the last year to revise and, in parts, re-write it. The great interest of it is that it belongs to a different age of the human mind, in which there is so much like and also unlike ourselves. Many of our commonplaces and common words are being thought out for the first time by Plato. Add to this that in the original this book is the most perfect work of art in the world. I wonder whether it will have any meaning or interest for you.

You asked me once whether I desired to make a Sister of Charity of you. Certainly not (although there are worse occupations); nor do I desire to make anything. But your talking about plans of life does lead me to think of what would be best and happiest for you. I do not object to the hunting and going to Florence and Rome, but should there not be some higher end to which these are the steps? I think that you might happily fill up a great portion of your life with literature (I am convinced that you have considerable talent and might become eminent) and a small portion with works of benevolence, just to keep us in love and charity with our poor neighbours; and the rest I do not grudge to society and hunting. Do you think that I am a hard taskmaster? Not very, I think. More especially as you will not be led away by my good advice. You see that I cannot bear to think of you

*Plato's *Republic*.

hunting and ballet-dancing when you are "fair, fat and forty-five." Do prepare yourself for that awful age.

I went to see Mrs. H. Ward the other day: she insists on doing battle with the reviewer in the *Quarterly*, and is thinking of another novel, of which the subject will be the free-thinking of honest working-men in Paris and elsewhere. People say that in *Robert Elsmere* Rose is intended for you, Catherine for your sister Laura, the Squire for Mark Pattison, the Provost for me, etc., and Mr. Grey for Professor Green. All the portraits are about equally unlike the originals.

Good-bye, you have been sitting with me for nearly an hour, and now, like Laodamia or Protesilaus, you disappear. I have been the better for your company. One serious word: May God bless you and help you in this and every other great hurt of life.

Ever yours,<br>B. JOWETT.

I will publish all his letters to me together, as, however delightful letters may be, I find they bore me when they are scattered all through an autobiography.

*March 11th,* 1889.

MY DEAR MARGARET,

As you say, friendships grow dull if two persons do not care to write to one another. I was beginning to think that you resented my censorious criticisms on your youthful life and happiness.

[110]

# AN AUTOBIOGRAPHY

Can youth be serious without ceasing to be youth? I think it may. The desire to promote the happiness of others rather than your own may be always "breaking in." As my poor sister (of whom I will talk to you some day) would say: "When others are happy, then I am happy." She used to commend the religion of Sydney Smith—"Never to let a day pass without doing a kindness to some body" —and I think that you understand something about this; or you would not be so popular and beloved.

You ask me what persons I have seen lately: I doubt whether they would interest you. Mr. Welldon, the Headmaster of Harrow, a very honest and able man with a long life before him, and if he is not too honest and open, not unlikely to be an Archbishop of Canterbury. Mr. J. M. Wilson, Headmaster of Clifton College—a very kind, genial and able man—there is a great deal of him and in him—not a man of good judgment, but very devoted—a first-rate man in his way. Then I have seen a good deal of Lord Rosebery—very able, shy, sensitive, ambitious, the last two qualities rather at war with each other—very likely a future Prime Minister. I like Lady Rosebery too—very sensible and high-principled, not at all inclined to give up her Judaism to please the rest of the world. They are rather overloaded with wealth and fine houses: they are both very kind. I also like Lady Leconfield,* whom I saw at Mentone. Then I paid a visit to Tennyson, who has had a lingering illness of six months, perhaps fatal, as he is eighty years

*Lady Leconfield was a sister of Lord Rosebery's and one of my dearest friends.

of age. It was pleasing to see how he takes it, very patient and without fear of death, unlike his former state of mind. Though he is so sensitive, he seemed to me to bear his illness like a great man. He has a volume of poems waiting to come out—some of them as good as he ever wrote. Was there ever an octogenarian poet before?

Doctor Johnson used to say that he never in his life had eaten as much fruit as he desired. I think I never talked to you as much as I desired. You once told me that you would show me your novel.* Is it a reality or a myth? I should be interested to see it if you like to send me that or any other writing of yours.

*Robert Elsmere*, as the authoress tells me, has sold 60,000 in England and 400,000 in America! It has considerable merit, but its success is really due to its saying what everybody is thinking. I am astonished at her knowing so much about German theology—she is a real scholar and takes up things of the right sort. I do not believe that Mrs. Ward ever said "she had pulverised Christianity." These things are invented about people by the orthodox, i. e., the infidel world, in the hope that they will do them harm. What do you think of being "laughed to death"? It would be like being tickled to death.

Good-bye,

Ever yours truly,

B. JOWETT.

*I began two, but they were not at all clever and have long since disappeared.

[112]

LORD MIDLETON, BETTER KNOWN AS ST. JOHN BRODRICK:
FORMER SECRETARY OF STATE FOR WAR

JOHN ADDINGTON SYMONDS,
WHO ENCOURAGED MARGOT'S
LITERARY ENDEAVOURS

# AN AUTOBIOGRAPHY

BALLIOL COLLEGE,
*May 22nd,* 1891.

MY DEAR MARGARET,

It was very good of you to write me such a nice note. I hope you are better. I rather believe in people being able to cure themselves of many illnesses if they are tolerably prudent and have a great spirit.

I liked your two friends who visited me last Sunday, and shall hope to make them friends of mine. Asquith is a capital fellow, and has abilities which may rise to the highest things in the law and politics. He is also very pleasant socially. I like your lady friend. She has both "Sense and Sensibility," and is free from "Pride and Prejudice." She told me that she had been brought up by an Evangelical grandmother, and is none the worse for it.

I begin to think bed is a very nice place, and I see a great deal of it, not altogether from laziness, but because it is the only way in which I am able to work.

I have just read the life of Newman, who was a strange character. To me he seems to have been the most artificial man of our generation, full of ecclesiastical loves and hatred. Considering what he really was, it is wonderful what a space he has filled in the eyes of mankind. In speculation he was habitually untruthful and not much better in practice. His conscience had been taken out, and the Church put in its place. Yet he was a man of genius, and a good man in the sense of being disinterested. Truth is very often troublesome, but

[113]

neither the world nor the individual can get on without it.

Here is the postman appearing at 12 o'clock, as disagreeable a figure as the tax-gatherer.

May you have good sleep and pleasant dreams. I shall still look forward to seeing you with Lady Wemyss.

Believe me always,

Yours affectionately,

B. JOWETT.

BALLIOL COLLEGE,
*Sep.* 8, 1892.

MY DEAR MARGARET,

Your kind letter was a very sweet consolation to me. It was like you to think of a friend in trouble.

Poor Nettleship, whom we have lost, was a man who cannot be replaced—certainly not in Oxford. He was a very good man, and had a considerable touch of genius in him. He seems to have died bravely, telling the guides not to be cowards, but to save their lives. He also sang to them to keep them awake, saying (this was so like him) that he had no voice, but that he would do his best. He probably sang that song of Salvator Rosa's which we have so often heard from him. He was wonderfully beloved by the undergraduates, because they knew that he cared for them more than for anything else in the world.

Of his writings there is not much, except what you have read, and a long essay on Plato in a book called *Hellenism*—very good. He was beginning to write, and I think would have written well. He

was also an excellent speaker and lecturer—Mr.
Asquith would tell you about him.

I have received many letters about him—but
none of them has touched me as much as yours.
Thank you, dear.

I see that you are in earnest about writing—no
slipshod or want of connection. Writing requires
boundless leisure, and is an infinite labour, yet there
is also a very great pleasure in it. I shall be delighted to read your sketches.

BALLIOL COLLEGE,
*Dec. 27th,* 1892.

MY DEAR MARGARET,

I have been reading Lady Jeune's two articles.
I am glad that you did not write them and have
never written anything of that sort. These criticisms on Society in which some of us "live and move
and have our being" are mistaken. In the first
place, the whole fabric of society is a great mystery,
with which we ought not to take liberties, and which
should be spoken of only in a whisper when we com-
pare our experiences, whether in a walk or *tête-à-
tête,* or "over the back hair" with a faithful, reserved
confidante. And there is also a great deal that is
painful in the absence of freedom in the division of
ranks, and the rising or falling from one place in
it to another. I am convinced that it is a thing not
to be spoken of; what we can do to improve it or
do it good—whether I, the head of a college at Oxford, or a young lady of fashion (I know that you
don't like to be called *that*)—must be done quite
silently.

[115]

Lady Jeune believes that all the world would go right, or at least be a great deal better, if it were not for the Nouveaux Riches. Some of the Eton masters talk to me in the same way. I agree with our dear friend, Lady Wemyss, that the truth is "the old poor are so jealous of them." We must study the arts of uniting Society as a whole, not clinging to any one class of it—what is possible and desirable to what is impossible and undesirable.

I hope you are none the worse for your great effort. You know it interests me to hear what you are about if you have time and inclination to write. I saw your friend, Mr. Asquith, last night: very nice and not at all puffed up with his great office.* The fortunes of the Ministry seem very doubtful. There is a tendency to follow Lord Rosebery in the Cabinet. Some think that the Home Rule Bill will be pushed to the second reading, then dropped, and a new shuffle of the cards will take place under Lord Rosebery: this seems to me very likely. The Ministry has very little to spare and they are not gaining ground, and the English are beginning to hate the Irish and the Priests.

I hope that all things go happily with you. Tell me some of your thoughts. I have been reading Mr. Milner's book with great satisfaction—most interesting and very important. I fear that I have written you a dull and meandering epistle.

Ever yours,

B. Jowett.

*The Home Office.

# AN AUTOBIOGRAPHY

BALLIOL COLLEGE,
*Feb.* 13, 1893.

MY DEAR MARGARET,

I began at ten minutes to twelve last night to write to you, but as the postman appeared at five minutes to twelve, it was naturally cut short. May I begin where I left off? I should like to talk to you about many things. I hope you will not say, as Johnson says to Boswell, "Sir, you have only two subjects, yourself and me, and I am heartily sick of both."

I have been delighted with Mr. Asquith's success. He has the certainty of a great man in him—such strength and simplicity and independence and superiority to the world and the clubs. You seem to me very fortunate in having three such friends as Mr. Asquith, Mr. Milner and Mr. Balfour. I believe that you may do a great deal for them, and they are probably the first men of their time, or not very far short of it.

Mr. Balfour is not so good a leader of the House of Commons in opposition as he was when he was in office. He is too aggressive and not dignified enough. I fear that he will lose weight. He had better not coquette with the foolish and unpractical thing "Bimetallism," or write books on "Philosophic Doubt"; for there are many things which we must certainly believe, are there not? Quite enough either for the highest idealism or for ordinary life. He will probably, like Sir R. Peel, have to change many of his opinions in the course of the next thirty years and he should be on his guard about this, or he will commit himself in such a manner that he may

[117]

have to withdraw from politics (about the currency, about the Church, about Socialism).

Is this to be the last day of Gladstone's life in the House of Commons? It is very pathetic to think of the aged man making his last great display almost in opposition to the convictions of his whole life. I hope that he will acquit himself well and nobly, and then it does not much matter whether or no he dies like Lord Chatham a few days afterwards. It seems to me that his Ministry have not done badly during the last fortnight. They have, to a great extent, removed the impression they had created in England that they were the friends of disorder. Do you know, I cannot help feeling I have more of the Liberal element in me than of the Conservative? This rivalry between the parties, each surprising the other by their liberality, has done a great deal of good to the people of England.

HEADINGTON HILL,
near OXFORD,
*July 30th,* 1893.

MY DEAR MARGARET,
Did you ever read these lines?—

'Tis said that marriages are made above—
It may be so, some few, perhaps, for love.
But from the smell of sulphur I should say
They must be making *matches* here all day.

(Orpheus returning from the lower world in a farce called *The Olympic Devils,* which used to be played when I was young.)

[118]

Miss Nightingale talks to me of "the feelings usually called love," but then she is a heroine, perhaps a goddess.

This love-making is a very serious business, though society makes fun of it, perhaps to test the truth and earnestness of the lovers.

Dear, I am an old man, what the poet calls "on the threshold of old age" (Homer), and I am not very romantic or sentimental about such things, but I would do anything I could to save any one who cares for me from making a mistake.

I think that you are quite right in not running the risk without a modest abode in the country.

The real doubt about the affair is the family; will you consider this and talk it over with your mother? The other day you were at a masqued ball, as you told me—a few months hence you will have, or rather may be having, the care of five children, with all the ailments and miseries and disagreeables of children (unlike the children of some of your friends) and not your own, although you will have to be a mother to them, and this state of things will last during the greatest part of your life. Is not the contrast more than human nature can endure? I know that it is, as you said, a nobler manner of living, but are you equal to such a struggle. If you are, I can only say, "God bless you, you are a brave girl." But I would not have you disguise from yourself the nature of the trial. It is not possible to be a leader of fashion and to do your duty to the five children.

On the other hand, you have at your feet a man of outstanding ability and high character, and who

[119]

has attained an extraordinary position—far better than any aristocratic lath or hop-pole; and you can render him the most material help by your abilities and knowledge of the world. Society will be gracious to you because you are a *grata persona,* and everybody will wish you well because you have made the sacrifice. You may lead a much higher life if you are yourself equal to it.

To-day I read Hume's life—by himself—very striking. You will find it generally at the beginning of his History of England. There have been saints among infidels too, e.g., Hume and Spinoza, on behalf of whom I think it a duty to say something as the Church has devoted them to eternal flames. To use a German phrase, "They were 'Christians in unconsciousness.' " That describes a good many people. I believe that as Christians we should get rid of a good many daubtful phrases and speak only through our lives.

Believe me, my dear Margaret,

Yours truly and affectionately,

B. JOWETT.

BALLIOL,
*Sunday.* 1893.

MY DEAR MARGARET,

I quite agree with you that what we want most in life is rest and peace. To act up to our best lights, that is quite enough; there need be no trouble about dogmas, which are hardly intelligible to us, nor ought there to be any trouble about historical facts, including miracles, of which the view of the world has naturally altered in the course of ages.

[120]

I include in this such questions as whether Our Lord rose from the dead in any natural sense of the words. It is quite a different question, whether we shall imitate Him in His life.

I am glad you think about these questions, and shall be pleased to talk to you about them. What I have to say about religion is contained in two words: Truth and Goodness, but I would not have one without the other, and if I had to choose between them, might be disposed to give Truth the first place. I think, also, that you might put religion in another way, as absolute resignation to the Will of God and the order of nature. There might be other definitions, equally true, but none suited better than another to the characters of men, such as the imitation of Christ, or the truth in all religions, which would be an adequate description of it. The Christian religion seems to me to extend to all the parts and modes of life, and then to come back to our hearts and conscience. I think that the best way of considering it, and the most interesting, is to view it as it may be seen in the lives of good men everywhere, whether Christians or so-called heathens—Socrates, Plato, Marcus Aurelius, St. Augustine, as well as in the lives of Christ, or Bunyan, or Spinoza. The study of religious biography seems to me one of the best modes of keeping up Christian feeling.

As to the question of Disestablishment, I am not like Mr. Balfour, I wobble rather, yet, on the whole, I agree with Mr. Gladstone, certainly about the Welsh Church. Churches are so worldly and so much allied to the interests of the higher classes. I think that a person who belongs to a Church should always endeavour to live above his Church, above the sermon and a good part of the prayer, above the Athanasian Creed, and the form of Ordination, above the passions of party feelings and public meetings. The best individuals have always been better than Churches, though I do not go so far as a German professor, who thinks that people will never be religious until they leave off going to church, yet I am of opinion that in every congregation the hearers should attempt to raise themselves above the tone of the preacher and of the service.

I am sorry to hear that Mr. Balfour, who has so much that is liberal in him, is of an extreme opposite opinion. But I feel that I have talked long enough on a subject which may not interest you, but of which I should like to talk to you again when we meet. It seems to me probable that the Church *will* be disestablished, because it has been so already in most countries of Europe, and because the school is everywhere taking its place.

I shall look forward to your coming to see me, if I am seriously ill—"Be with me when my light is low." But I don't think that this illness which I at present have is serious enough to make any of my friends anxious, and it would be rather awkward for my friends to come and take leave of me if I recovered, which I mean to do, for what I think a good reason—because I *still* have a good deal to do.

B. JOWETT.

My beloved friend died in 1893.

The year before his death he had the dangerous

illness to which he alludes in the above letter. Every one thought he would die. He dictated farewell letters to all his friends by his secretary and housekeeper, Miss Knight. On receiveing mine from him at Glen, I was so much annoyed at its tone that I wired:

Jowett Balliol College Oxford.
I refuse to accept this as your farewell letter to me you have been listening to some silly woman and believing what she says. Love.

MARGOT.

This telegram had a magical effect: he got steadily better and wrote me a wonderful letter. I remember the reason that I was vexed was because he believed a report that I had knocked up against a foreign potentate in Rotten Row for a bet, which was not only untrue but ridiculous, and I was getting a little impatient of the cattishness and credulity of the West-end of London.

My week-ends at Balliol were different to my other visits. The Master took infinite trouble over them. Once on my arrival he asked me which of one or two men I would like to sit next to at dinner. I said I should prefer Mr. Huxley or Lord Bowen, to which he replied:

"I would like you to have on your other side, either to-night or to-morrow, my friend Lord Selborne*:

MARGOT (*with surprise*): "Since when is he your friend? I was under the impression you disliked him."

JOWETT: "Your impression was right, but even the youngest of us are sometimes wrong, as Dr. Thompson said, and I look upon Lord Selborne now as a friend. I hope I said nothing against him."

MARGOT: "Oh dear no! You only said he was fond of hymns and had no sense of humour."

JOWETT (*snappishly*): "If that is so, Margaret, I made an extremely foolish remark. I will put you between Lord Bowen and Sir Alfred Lyall. Was it not strange that you should have said of Lyall to Huxley that he reminded you of a faded Crusader and that you suspected him of wearing a coat of mail under his broadcloth, to which you will remember Huxley remarked, 'You mean a coating of female, without which no man is saved!' Your sister, Lady Ribblesdale, said the very same thing to me about him."

*The late Earl of Selborne.

This interested me, as Charty and I had not spoken to each other of Sir Alfred Lyall, who was a new acquaintance of ours.

MARGOT: "I am sure, Master, you did not give her the same answer as Mr. Huxley gave me; you don't think well of my sex, do you?"

JOWETT: "You are not the person to reproach me, Margaret: only the other week I reproved you for saying women were often dull, sometimes dangerous and always dishonourable. I might have added they were rarely reasonable and always courageous. Would you agree to this?"

MARGOT: "Yes."

I sat between Sir Alfred Lyall and Lord Bowen that night at dinner. There was more bouquet than body about Sir Alfred and, to parody Gibbon, Lord Bowen's mind was not clouded by enthusiasm; but two more delightful men never existed. After dinner, Huxley came across the room to me and said that the Master had confessed he had done him out of sitting next to me, so would I talk to him? We sat down together and our conversation opened on religion.

There was not much *juste milieu* about Huxley. He began by saying God was only there because people believed in Him, and that the fastidious incognito, "I am that I am," was His idea of humour, etc., etc. He ended by saying he did not believe any man of action had ever been inspired by religion. I thought I would call in Lord Bowen, who was standing aimlessly in the middle of the room, to my assistance. He instantly responded and drew a chair up to us. I said to him:

"Mr. Huxley challenges me to produce any man of action who has been directly inspired by religion."

BOWEN (*with a sleek smile*): "Between us we should be able to answer him, Miss Tennant, I think. Who is your man?"

Every idea seemed to scatter out of my brain. I suggested at random:

"Gordon."

I might have been reading his thoughts, for it so happened that Huxley adored General Gordon.

HUXLEY: "Ah! There you rather have me!"

He had obviously had enough of me, for, changing the position of his chair, as if to engage Bowen in a *tête-à-tête,* he said:

"My dear Bowen, Gordon was the most remarkable man I ever met. I know him well; he was sincere and disinterested, quite incapable of saying anything he did not think. You will hardly believe me, but one day he said in tones of passionate conviction that, if he were to walk round the corner of the street and have his brains shot out, he would only be transferred to a wider sphere of government."

BOWEN: "Would the absence of brains have been of any help to him?"

After this, our mutual good humour was restored and I only had time for a word with Mrs. Green before the evening was ruined by Jowett taking us across the quad to hear moderate music in the hideous Balliol hall. Of all the Master's women friends, I infinitely preferred Mrs. T. H. Green, John Addington Symonds' sister. She is among the rare women who have all the qualities which in moments of disillusion I deny to them.

I spent my last week-end at Balliol when Jowett's health appeared to have completely recovered. On the Monday morning, after his guests had gone, I went as usual into his study to talk to him. My wire on receiving his death-bed letter had amused but distressed him; and on my arrival he pressed me to tell him what it was he had written that had offended me. I told him I was not offended, only hurt. He asked me what the difference was. I wish I could have given him the answer that my daughter Elizabeth gave Lord Grey* when he asked her the same question, walking in the garden at Fallodon on the occasion of her first country-house visit:

"The one touches your vanity and the other your heart."

I do not know what I said, but I told him I was quite unoffended and without touchiness, but that his letter had all the faults of a schoolmaster and a cleric in it and not the love of a friend. He listened to me with his usual patience and sweetness and expressed his regret.

On the Monday morning of which I am writing, and on which we had our last conversation, I had made up my mind that, as I had spoilt many good conversations by talking too much myself, I would hold my tongue and let the Master for once make the first move. I had not had much experience of his classical and devastating silences and had often defended him from the charge; but it was time to see what happened if I talked less.

*Viscount Grey of Fallodon.

When we got into the room and he had shut the door, I absently selected the only comfortable chair and we sat down next to each other. A long and quelling silence followed the lighting of my cigarette. Feeling rather at a loose end, I thought out a few stage directions—"here business with handkerchief, etc."—and adjusted the buckles on my shoes. I looked at some photographs and fingered a paper-knife and odds and ends on the table near me. The oppressive silence continued. I strolled to the book-shelves and, under cover of a copy of *Country Conversations,* peeped at the Master. He appeared to be quite unaware of my existence.

"Nothing doing," said I to myself, putting back the book.

Something had switched him off as if he had been the electric light.

At last, breaking the silence with considerable impatience, I said:

"Really, Master, there is very little excuse for your silence! Surely you have something to say to me, something to tell me; you have had an experience since we talked to each other that I have never had: you have been near Death."

JOWETT (*not in any way put out*): "I felt no rapture, no bliss." (*Suddenly looking at me and taking my hand.*) "My dear child, you must believe in God in spite of what the clergy say."

# CHAPTER III

FAST AND FURIOUS HUNTING IN LEICESTERSHIRE—
COUNTRY HOUSE PARTY AND A NEW ADMIRER—
FRIENDSHIP WITH LORD AND LADY MANNERS

MY friendship with Lord and Lady Manners,* of Avon Tyrrell, probably made more difference to the course of my life than anything that had happened in it.

Riding was what I knew and cared most about; and I dreamt of High Leicestershire. I had hunted in Cheshire, where you killed three foxes a day and found yourself either clattering among cottages and clothes-lines, or blocked by carriages and crowds; I knew the stiff plough and fine horses of Yorkshire and the rotten grass in the Bicester; I had struggled over the large fences and small enclosures of the Grafton and been a heroine in the select fields and large becks with the Burton; and the Beaufort had seen the dawn of my fox-hunting; but Melton was a name which brought the Hon. Crasher before me

*Avon Tyrrell, Christchurch, Hants. Lady Manners was a Miss Fane.

and opened a vista on my future of all that was fast, furious and fashionable.

When I was told that I was going to sit next to the Master of the Quorn at dinner, my excitement knew no bounds.

Gordon Cunard—whose brother Bache owned the famous hounds in Market Harborough—had insisted on my joining him at a country-house party given for a ball. On getting the invitation I had refused, as I hardly knew our hostess—the pretty Mrs. Farnham—but after receiving a spirited telegram from my new admirer—one of the best men to hounds in Leicestershire—I changed my mind. In consequence of this decision a double event took place. I fell in love with Peter Flower—a brother of the late Lord Battersea—and formed an attachment with a couple whose devotion and goodness to me for more than twenty years encouraged and embellished my glorious youth.

Lord Manners, or "Hoppy," as we called him, was one of the few men I ever met whom the word "single-minded" described. His sense of honour was only equalled by his sense of humour; and a more original, tender, truthful, uncynical, real being never existed. He was a fine sportsman and had won the Grand Military when he was in the Grenadiers, riding one of his own hunters; he was also the second gentleman in England to win the Grand National in 1882, on a thoroughbred called Seaman, who was by no means every one's horse. For other people he cared nothing. *"Décidément je n'aime pas les autres,"* he would have said, to quote my son-in-law, Antoine Bibesco.

His wife often said that, but for her, he would not have asked a creature inside the house; be this as it may, no host and hostess could have been more socially susceptible or given their guests a warmer welcome than Con and Hoppy Manners.

What I loved and admired in him was his keenness and his impeccable unworldliness. He was perfectly independent of public opinion and as free from rancour as he was from fear, malice or acerbity. He never said a stupid thing. Some people would say that this is not a compliment, but the amount of silly things that I have heard clever people say makes me often wonder what is left for the stupid.

His wife was very different, though quite as free from rhetoric.

Under a becalmed exterior Con Manners was a

little brittle and found it difficult to say she was in the wrong; this impenitence caused some of her lovers a suffering of which she was unconscious; it is a minor failing which strikes a dumb note in me, but which I have since discovered is not only common, but almost universal. I often warned people of Con's dangerous smile when I observed them blundering along; but though she was uneven in her powers of forgiveness, the serious quarrel of her life was made up ultimately without reserve. Lady Manners was clever, gracious, and understanding; she was more worldly, more adventurous and less deprecating than her husband; people meant a great deal to her; and the whole of London was at her feet, except those lonely men and women who specialise in collecting the famous as men collect centipedes.

To digress here, I asked my friend Mr. Birrell once how the *juste milieu* was to be found—for an enterprising person—between running after the great men of the day and missing them; and he said:

"I would advise you to live among your superiors, Margot, but to be of them."

Con was one of the few women of whom it could

be said that she was in an equal degree a wonderful wife, mother, sister and friend. Her charm of manner and the tenderness of her *regard* gave her face beauty that was independent—almost a rival of fine features—and she was a saint of goodness.

Her love of flowers made every part of her home, inside and out, radiant; and her sense of humour and love of being entertained stimulated the witty and the lazy.

For nineteen years I watched her go about her daily duties with a quiet grace and serenity infinitely restful to live with, and when I was separated from her it nearly broke my heart. In connection with the love Con and I had for each other I will only add an old French quotation:

*"Par grace infinie Dieu les mist au monde ensemble."*

My dear friend, Mrs. Hamlyn, was the châtelaine of the famous Clovelly, in Devonshire, and was Con's sister. She had the spirit of eternal youth and was full of breathless admiration. I hardly ever met any one who derived so much pleasure and surprise out of ordinary life. She was as uncritical and tolerant of those she loved as she was narrow and vehement over those who had unaccountably offended her. She had an ebullient and voracious sense of humour and was baffled and *éblouie* by titled people, however vulgar and ridiculous they might be. By this I do not mean she was a snob— on the contrary she made and kept friends among the frumps and the obscure, to whom she showed faithful hospitality; but she was old-fashioned and thought that all duchesses were ladies.

Christine Hamlyn was a character-part; but, if the machinery was not invented by which you could remove her prejudices, no tank could turn her from her friends. It was through the Souls and these friends whom I have endeavoured to describe that I entered into a new phase of my life.

# CHAPTER IV

MARGOT FALLS IN LOVE AGAIN—"HAVOC" IN THE
HUNTING FIELD; A FALL AND A DUCKING—THE
FAMOUS MRS. BO; UNHEEDED ADVICE FROM A
RIVAL—A LOVERS' QUARREL—PETER JUMPS IN
THE WINDOW—THE AMERICAN TROTTER—AN-
OTHER LOVER INTERVENES—PETER RETURNS
FROM INDIA; ILLUMINATION FROM A DARK
WOMAN

THE first time I ever saw Peter Flower was at
Ranelagh, where he had taken my sister
Charty Ribblesdale to watch a polo-match. They
were sitting together at an iron table, under a cedar
tree, eating ices. I was wearing a grey muslin dress
with a black sash and a black hat, with coral beads
round my throat, and heard him say as I came up
to them:

"Nineteen? Not possible! I should have said
fifteen! Is that the one that rides so well?"

After shaking hands I sat down and looked about
me.

I always notice what men wear; and Peter
Flower was the best-dressed man I had ever seen.

[137]

I do not know who could have worn his clothes when they were new; but certainly he never did. After his clothes, what I was most struck by was his peculiar, almost animal grace, powerful sloping shoulders, fascinating laugh and infectious vitality.

Laurence Oliphant once said to me, "I divide the world into life-givers and life-takers"; and I have often had reason to feel the truth of this, being as I am acutely sensitive to high spirits. On looking back along the gallery of my acquaintance, I can find not more than three or four people as tenacious of life as Peter was: Lady Desborough, Lady Cunard, my son Anthony and myself. There are various kinds of high spirits: some so crude and rough-tongued that they vitiate what they touch and estrange every one of sensibility and some so insistent that they tire and suffocate you; but Peter's vitality revived and restored every one he came in contact with; and, when I said good-bye to him that day at Ranelagh, although I cannot remember a single sentence of any interest spoken by him or by me, my mind was absorbed in thinking of when and how I could meet him again.

In the winter of that same year I went with the Ribblesdales to stay with Peter's brother, Lord

Battersea, to have a hunt. I took with me the best of hats and habits and two leggy and faded hirelings, hoping to pick up a mount. Charty having twisted her knee the day after we arrived, this enabled me to ride the horse on which Peter was to have mounted her; and full of spirits we all went off to the meet of the Bicester hounds. I had hardly spoken three words to my benefactor, but Ribblesdale had rather unwisely told him that I was the best rider to hounds in England.

At the meet I examined my mount closely while the man was lengthening my stirrup. Havoc, as he was called, was a dark chestnut, 16.1, with a coat like the back of a violin and a spiteful little head. He had an enormous bit on; and I was glad to see a leather strap under the curb-chain.

When I was mounted, Peter kept close to my side and said:

"You're on a topper! Take him where you like, but ride your own line."

To which I replied:

"Why? Does he rush? I had thought of following you."

PETER: "Not at all, but he may pull you a bit, so keep away from the field; the fence isn't made that he can't jump; and as for water, he's a swallow! I wish I could say the same of mine! We've got a brook round about here with rotten banks, it will catch the best! But, if we are near each other, you must come alongside and go first and mine will very likely follow you. I don't want to spend the night in that beastly brook."

It was a good scenting day and we did not take long to find. I stuck to Peter Flower while the Bicester hounds raced across the heavy grass towards a hairy-looking ugly double. In spite of the ironmonger's shop in Havoc's mouth, I had not the faintest control over him, so I said to Peter:

"You know, Mr. Flower, *I* can't stop your horse!"

He looked at me with a charming smile and said: "But why should you? Hounds are running!"

MARGOT: "But I can't turn him!"

PETER: "It doesn't matter! They are running straight. Hullo! Look out! Look out for Hydy!"

We were going great guns. I saw a man in front of me slowing up to the double, so shouted at him:

"Get out of my way! Get out of my way!"

I was certain that at the pace he was going he would take a heavy fall and I should be on the top of him. While in the act of turning round to see who it was that was shouting, his willing horse paused and I shot past him, taking away his spur in my habit skirt. I heard a volley of oaths as I jumped into the jungle. Havoc, however, did not like the brambles and, steadying himself as he landed, arched with the activity of a cat over a high rail on the other side of the double; I turned round and saw Peter's horse close behind me hit the rail and peck heavily upon landing, at which Peter gave him one down the shoulder and looked furious.

I had no illusions! I was on a horse that nothing could stop! Seeing a line of willows in front of me, I shouted to Peter to come along, as I thought if the brook was ahead of us I could not possibly keep close to him, going at that pace. To my surprise and delight, as we approached the willows Peter passed me and the water widened out in front of us; I saw by his set face that it was neck or nothing with him. Havoc was going well within himself, but his stable-companion was precipitate and flurried; and before I knew what had happened Peter was in the middle of the brook and I was jumping over his head. On landing I made a large circle round the field away from hounds, trying to pull up; and when I could turn round I found myself facing the brook again, with Peter dripping on the bank nearest to me. Havoc pricked his ears, passed him like a flash and jumped the brook again; but the bank on landing was boggy and while we were floundering I got a pull at him by putting the curb-rein under my pommel and, exhausted and distressed, I jumped off. Peter burst out laughing.

"We seem to be separated for life," he said. "Do look at my damned horse!"

I looked down the water and saw the animal standing knee-deep, nibbling grass and mud off the bank with perfect composure.

MARGOT: "I really believe Havoc would jump this brook for a third time and then I should be by your side. What luck that you aren't soaked to the skin; hadn't I better look out for the second horsemen? Hounds by now will be at the sea and I confess I can't ride your horse: does he always pull like this?"

PETER: "Yes, he catches hold a bit, but what do you mean? You rode him beautifully. Hullo! What is that spur doing in your skirt?"

MARGOT: "I took it off the man that you call

'Hydy,' who was going so sticky at the double when we started."

PETER: "Poor old Clarendon! I advise you to keep his spur, he'll never guess who took it; and, if I know anything about him, there will be no love lost between you even if you do return it to him!"

I was longing for another horse, as I could not bear the idea of going home. At that moment a single file of second horse-men came in sight; and Peter's well-trained servant, on a thoroughbred grey, rode up to us at the conventional trot. Peter lit a cigar and, pointing to the brook, said to his man:

"Go off and get a rope and hang that brute! Or haul him out, will you? And give me my lunch."

We were miles away from any human habitation and I felt depressed.

"Perhaps I had better ride home with your man," said I, looking tentatively at Peter.

"Home! What for?" said he.

MARGOT: "Are you sure Havoc is not tired?"

PETER: "I wish to God he was! But I daresay this infernal Bicester grass, which is heavier than anything I saw in Yorkshire, has steadied him a bit; you'll see he'll go far better with you this afternoon. I'm awfully sorry and would put you on my second horse, but it isn't mine and I'm told it's got a bit of a temper; if you go through that gate we'll have our lunch together. . . . Have a cigarette?"

I smiled and shook my head; my mouth was as dry as a Japanese toy and I felt shattered with fatigue. The ground on which I was standing was deep and I was afraid of walking in case I should leave my boots in it, so I tapped the back of Havoc's fetlocks till I got him stretched and with great skill mounted myself. This filled Peter with admiration; and, lifting his hat, he said:

"Well! You are the very first woman I ever saw mount herself without two men and a boy hanging on to the horse's head."

I rode towards the gate and Peter joined me a few minutes later on his second horse. He praised my riding and promised he would mount me any day in the week if I could only get some one to ask me down to Brackley where he kept his horses; he said the Grafton was the country to hunt in and that, though Tom Firr, the huntsman of the Quorn, was the greatest man in England, Frank Beers was hard to beat. I felt pleased at his admiration for

VISCOUNT GREY OF FALLODON, FRIEND OF THE ASQUITH FAMILY
AND SECRETARY OF STATE FOR FOREIGN AFFAIRS WHEN
ENGLAND SENT THE ULTIMATUM TO
GERMANY IN 1914

my riding, but I knew Havoc had not turned a hair and that, if I went on hunting, I should kill either myself, Peter on some one else.

"Aren't you nervous when you see a helpless woman riding one of your horses?" I said to him.

PETER: "No, I am only afraid she'll hurt my horse! I take her off pretty quick, I can tell you, if I think she's going to spoil my sale; but I never mount a woman. Your sister is a magnificent rider, or I would never have put her on that horse. Now come along and with any luck you will be alone with hounds this afternoon and Havoc will be knocked down at Tattersalls for five hundred guineas."

MARGOT: "You are sure you want me to go on?"

PETER: "You think I want you to go home? Very well! If you go . . . *I* go!"

I longed to have the courage to say, "Let us both go home," but I knew he would think that I was funking and it was still early in the day. He looked at me steadily and said:

"I will do exactly what you like."

I looked at him, but at that moment the hounds came in sight and my last chance was gone. We shogged along to the next cover, Havoc as mild as milk. I was amazed at Peter's nerve: if any horse of mine had taken such complete charge of its rider, I should have been in a state of anguish till I had separated them; but he was riding along talking and laughing in front of me in the highest of spirits. This lack of sensitiveness irritated me and my heart sank. Before reaching the cover, Peter came up to me and suggested that we should change Havoc's bit. I then perceived he was not quite so happy as I thought; and this determined me to stick it out. I thanked him demurely and added, with a slight and smiling shrug:

"I fear no bit can save me to-day, thank you."

At which Peter said with visible irritability:

"Oh, for God's sake then don't let us go on! If you hate my horse I vote we go no farther!"

"What a cross man!" I said to myself, seeing him flushed and snappy; but a ringing "Halloa!" brought our deliberations to an abrupt end.

Havoc and I shot down the road, passing the blustering field; and, hopping over a gap, we found ourselves close to the hounds, who were running hell-for-leather towards a handsome country seat perched upon a hill. A park is what I hate most out hunting: hounds invariably lose the line, the field loses its way and I lose my temper.

I looked round to see if my benefactor was near me, but he was nowhere to be seen. Eight or ten hard riders were behind me; they shouted:

"Don't go into the wood! Turn to your left! Don't go into the wood!"

I saw a fancy gate of yellow polished oak in front of me, at the end of one of the grass rides in the wood, and what looked like lawns beyond. I was unable to turn to the left with my companions, but plunged into the trees where the hounds paused: not so Havoc, who, in spite of the deep ground, was still going great guns. A lady behind me, guessing what had happened, left her companions and managed somehow or other to pass me in the ride; and, as I approached the yellow gate, she was holding it open for me. I shouted my thanks to her and she shouted back:

"Get off when you stop!"

This was my fixed determination, as I had observed that Havoc's tongue was over the bit and he was not aware that any one was on his back, nor was he the least tired and no doubt would have jumped the yellow gate with ease.

After leaving my saviour I was joined by my former companions. The hounds had picked up again and we left the gate, the wood and the country seat behind us. Still going very strong, we all turned into a chalk field with a white road sunk between two high banks leading down to a ford. I kept on the top of the bank, as I was afraid of splashing people in the water, if not knocking them down. Two men were standing by the fence ahead, which separated me from what appeared to be a river; and I knew there must be a considerable drop in front of me. They held their hands up in warning as I came galloping up; I took my foot out of the stirrup and dropping my reins gave myself up for lost, but in spite of Havoc slowing up he was going too fast to stop or turn. He made a magnificent effort, but I saw the water twinkling below me; and after that I knew no more.

When I came to, I was lying on a box bed in a cottage, with Peter and the lady who had held the yellow gate kneeling by my side.

"I think you are mad to put any one on that horse!" I heard her say indignantly. "You know how often it has changed hands; and you yourself can hardly ride it."

Havoc had tried to scramble down the bank, which luckily for me had not been immediately under the fence, but it could not be done, so we took a somersault into the brook, most alarming for the people in the ford to see. However, as the water was deep where I landed, I was not hurt, but had fainted from fear and exhaustion.

Peter's misery was profound; ice-white and in an agony of fear, he was warming my feet with both his hands while I watched him quietly. I was taken home in a brougham by my kind friend, who turned out to be Mrs. Bunbury, a sister of John Watson, the Master of the Meath hounds, and the daughter of old Mr. Watson, the Master of the Carlow and the finest rider to hounds in England.

This was how Peter and I first came really to know each other; and after that it was only a question of time when our friendship developed into a serious love-affair. I stayed with Mrs. Bunbury in the Grafton country that winter for several weeks and was mounted by every one.

As Peter was a kind of hero in the hunting field and had never been known to mount a woman, I was the object of much jealousy. The first scene in my life occurred at Brackley, where he and a friend of his, called Hatfield Harter, shared a hunting box together.

There was a lady of charm and beauty in the vicinity who went by the name of Mrs. Bo. They said she had gone well to hounds in her youth, but I had never observed her jump a twig. She often joined us when Peter and I were changing horses and once or twice had ridden home with us. Peter did not appear to like her much, but I was too busy to notice this one way or the other. One day I said to him I thought he was rather snubby to her and added:

"After all, she must have been a very pretty woman when she was young and I don't think it's nice of you to show such irritation when she joins us."

PETER: "Do you call her old?"

MARGOT: "Well, oldish I should say. She must be over thirty, isn't she?"

PETER: "Do you call that old?"

MARGOT: "I don't know! How old are you, Peter?"

PETER: "I shan't tell you."

One day I rode back from hunting, having got wet to the skin. I had left the Bunbury brougham in Peter's stables but I did not like to go back in wet clothes; so, after seeing my horse comfortably gruelled, I walked up to the charming lady's house to borrow dry clothes. She was out, but her maid gave me a coat and skirt, which—though much too big—served my purpose.

After having tea with Peter, who was ill in bed, I drove up to thank the lady for her clothes. She was lying on a long, thickly pillowed couch, smoking a cigarette in a boudoir that smelt of violets. She greeted me coldly; and I was just going away when she threw her cigarette into the fire and, suddenly sitting very erect, said:

"Wait! I have something to say to you."

I saw by the expression on her face that I had no chance of getting away, though I was tired and felt at a strange disadvantage in my flowing skirts.

MRS. BO: "Does it not strike you that going to tea with a man who is in bed is a thing no one can do?"

MARGOT: "Going to see a man who is ill? No, certainly not!"

MRS. BO: Well, then let me tell you for your own information how it will strike other people. I am a much older woman than you and I warn you, you can't go on doing this sort of thing! Why should you come down here among all of us who are friends and make mischief and create talk?"

I felt chilled to the bone and, getting up, said:

"I think I had better leave you now, as I am tired and you are angry."

Mrs. Bo (*standing up and coming very close to me*): "Do you not know that I would nurse Peter Flower through yellow fever! But, though I have lived next door to him these last three years, I would never dream of doing what you have done to-day."

The expression on her face was so intense that I felt sorry for her and said as gently as I could:

"I do not see why you shouldn't! Especially if you are all such friends down here as you say you are. However, every one has a different idea of what is right and wrong. . . . I must go now!"

I was determined not to stay a moment longer and walked to the door, but she had lost her head and said in a hard, bitter voice:

"You say every one has a different idea of right and wrong, but I should say you have none!"

At this I left the room.

When I told Mrs. Bunbury what had happened, all she said was:

"Cat! She's jealous! Before you came down here, Peter Flower was in love with her."

This was a great shock to me and I determined I would leave the Grafton country, as I had already been away far too long from my own people; so I wrote to Peter saying I was sorry not to say good-bye to him, but that I had to go home. The next day was Sunday. I got my usual love-letter from Peter—who, whether I saw him or not, wrote daily—telling me that his temperature had gone up again and that he would give me his two best horses on Monday, as he was not allowed to leave his room. After we had finished lunch, Peter turned up, look-ing ill and furious. Mrs. Bunbury greeted him sweetly and said:

"You ought to be in bed, you know; but, since you *are* here, I'll leave Margot to look after you while Jacky and I go round the stables."

When we were left to ourselves, Peter, looking at me, said:

"Well! I've got your letter! What is all this about? Don't you know there are two horses coming over from Ireland this week which I want you particularly to ride for me?"

I saw that he was thoroughly upset and told him

[153]

that I was going home, as I had been already too long away.

"Have your people written to you?" he said.

MARGOT: "They always write. . . ."

PETER (*seeing the evasion*): "What's wrong?"

MARGOT: "What do you mean?"

PETER: "You know quite well that no one has asked you to go home. Something has happened; some one has said something to you; you've been put out. After all it was only yesterday that we were discussing every meet; and you promised to give me a lurcher. What has happened since to change you?"

MARGOT: "Oh, what does it matter? I can always come down here again later on."

PETER: "How wanting in candour you are! You are not a bit like what I thought you were!"

MARGOT (*sweetly*): "No. . . .?"

PETER: "Not a bit! You are a regular woman. I thought differently of you somehow!"

MARGOT: "You thought I was a dog-fancier or a rough-rider, did you, with a good thick skin?"

PETER: "I fail to understand you! Are you alluding to the manners of my horses?"

MARGOT: "No, to your friends."

[154]

PETER: "Ah! Ah! *Nous y sommes!* . . . How can you be so childish! What did Mrs. Bo say to you?"

MARGOT: "Oh, spare me from going into your friends' affairs!"

PETER (*flushed with temper, but trying to control himself*): "What does it matter what an old woman says whose nose has been put out of joint in the hunting-field?"

MARGOT: "You told me she was young."

PETER: "What an awful lie! You said she was pretty and I disagreed with you." Silence. "What did she say to you? I tell you she is jealous of you in the hunting-field!"

MARGOT: "No, she's not; she's jealous of me in your bedroom and says I don't know right from wrong."

PETER (*startled at first and then bursting out laughing*): "There's nothing very original about that!"

MARGOT (*indignantly*): "Do you mean to say that it's a platitude? And that I *don't* know right from wrong?"

PETER (*taking my hands and kissing them with a sigh of intense relief*): "I wonder!"

[155]

MARGOT (*getting up*): "Well, after that, nothing will induce me to stay down here or ride any of your horses ever again! No regiment of soldiers will keep me!"

PETER: "Really, darling, how can you be so foolish! Who would ever think it wrong to go and see a poor devil ill in bed! You had to ride my horse back to its stable and it was your duty to come and ask after me and thank me for all my kindness to you and the good horses I've put you on!"

MARGOT: "Evidently in this country I am not wanted, Mrs. Bo said so; and you ought to have warned me you were in love with her. You said I was not the woman you thought I was: well, I can say the same of you!"

At this Peter got up and all his laughter disappeared.

"Do you mean what you say? Is this the impression you got from talking to Mrs. Bo?"

MARGOT: "Yes."

PETER: "In that case I will go and see her and ask her which of the two of you is lying! If it's you, you needn't bother yourself to leave this country, for I shall sell my horses. . . . I wish to God I had never met you!"

I felt very uncomfortable and unhappy, as in my heart I knew that Mrs. Bo had never said Peter was in love with her; she had not alluded to his feelings for her at all. I got up to stop him leaving the room and put myself in front of the door.

MARGOT: "Really, why make scenes! There is nothing so tiring; and you know quite well you are ill and ought to go to bed. Is there any object in going round the country discussing me?"

PETER: "Just go away, will you? I'm ill and want to get off."

I did not move; I saw he was white with rage. The idea of going round the country talking about me was more than he could bear; so I said, trying to mollify him:

"If you want to discuss me, I am always willing to listen; there is nothing I enjoy so much as talking about myself."

It was too late. All he said to me was:

"Do you mind leaving that door? You tire me and it's getting dark."

MARGOT: "I will let you go, but promise me you won't go to Mrs. Bo to-day; or, if you *do,* tell me what you are going to say to her first."

PETER: "You've never told me yet what she said

to you, except that I was in love with her, so why should I tell you what I propose saying to her! For once you cannot have it all your own way. You are *so* spoilt since you've been down here that . . ."

I flung the door wide open and, before he could finish his sentence, ran up to my room.

. . . . . . .

Peter was curiously upsetting to the feminine sense; he wanted to conceal it and to expose it at the same time, under the impression it might arouse my jealousy. He was specially angry with me for dancing with King Edward, then the Prince of Wales. I told him that if he would learn to waltz instead of prance I would dance with him, but till he did I should choose my own partners. Over this we had a great row; and, after sitting out two dances with the Prince, I put on my cloak and walked round to 40 Grosvenor Square without saying good night to Peter. I was in my dressing-gown, with my hair—my one claim to beauty—standing out all round my head, when I heard a noise in the street and, looking down, I saw Peter standing on the wall of our porch gazing across an angle of the area into the open window of our library, contemplating, I presumed, jumping into

[158]

it; I raced downstairs to stop this dangerous folly, but I was too late and, as I opened the library-door, he had given a cat-like spring, knocking a flower-pot down into the area, and was by my side. I lit two candles on the writing-table and scolded him for his recklessness. He told me had made a great deal of money by jumping from a stand on to tables and things and once he had won £500 by jumping on to a mantelpiece when the fire was burning. As we were talking I heard voices in the area; Peter, with the instinct of a burglar, instantly lay flat on the floor behind the sofa, his head under the valance of the chintz, and I remained at the writing-table, smoking my cigarette; this was all done in a second. The door opened; I looked round and was blinded by the blaze of a bull's-eye lantern. When it was removed from my face, I saw two policemen, an inspector and my father's servant. I got up slowly and, with my head in the air, sat upon the arm of the sofa, blocking the only possibility of Peter's full length being seen.

MARGOT (*with great dignity*): "Is this a practical joke?"

INSPECTOR (*coolly*): "Not at all, madam, but it

[159]

is only right to tell you a hansom cabman informed us that, as he was passing this house a few minutes ago, he saw a man jump into that window."

He walked away from me and, holding his lantern over the area, peered down and saw the broken flower-pot. I knew lying was more than useless and, as the truth had always served me well, I said, giving my father's servant, who looked sleepy, a heavy kick on the instep:

"That is quite true; a friend of mine *did* jump in at that window, about a quarter of an hour ago; but (*looking down with a sweet and modest smile*) he was not a burglar. . . ."

HENRY HILL (*my father's servant*): "How often I've told you, miss, that, as long as Master Edward loses his latch-keys, there is nothing to be done and something is bound to happen! One day he will not only lose the latch-key, but his life."

INSPECTOR: "I'm sorry to have frightened you, madam, I will now take down your names. . . ."

MARGOT (*anxiously*): "Oh, I see, you have to report it in the police news, have you? Has the cabman given you his name? He ought to be rewarded, he might have saved us all!"

I felt that I could have strangled the cabman,

[160]

W. E. GLADSTONE, THE GREAT LIBERAL STATESMAN, WHOSE
NEPHEW, ARTHUR LYTTLETON, MARRIED LAURA
TENNANT, MARGOT'S SISTER

but, collecting myself, took one candle off the writing-table and, blowing the other out, led the way to the library-door, saying slowly:

"Margaret . . . Emma . . . Alice Tennant. Do I have to add my occupation?"

INSPECTOR (*busily writing in a small note-book*): "No, thank you." (*Turning to Hill*) "Your name, please."

My father's servant was thoroughly roused and I regretted my kick when in a voice of thunder he said:

"Henry Hastings Appleby Hill."

I felt quite sure that my father would appear over the top of the stair and then all would be over; but, by the fortune that follows the brave, perfect silence reigned throughout the house. I walked slowly away, while Hill led the three policemen into the hall. When the front door had been barred and bolted, I ran down the back stairs and said, smiling brightly:

"I shall tell my father all about this! You did very well; good night, Hill."

When the coast was clear, I returned to the library with my heart beating and shut the door. Peter had disentangled himself from the sofa and was taking fluff off his coat with an air of happy disengagement; I told him with emphasis that I was done for, that my name would be ringing in the police news next day and that I was quite sure by the inspector's face that he knew exactly what had happened; that all this came from Peter's infernal temper, idiotic jealousy and complete want of self-control. Agitated and eloquent, I was good for another ten minutes' abuse; but he interrupted me by saying, in his most caressing manner:

"The inspector is all right, my dear! He is a friend of mine! I wouldn't have missed this for the whole world: you were magnificent! Which shall we reward, the policeman, the cabman or Hill?"

MARGOT: "Don't be ridiculous! What do you propose doing?"

PETER (*trying to kiss my hands which I had purposely put behind my back*): "I propose having a chat with Inspector Wood and then with Hastings Appleby."

MARGOT: "How do you know Inspector Wood, as you call him?"

PETER: "He did a friend of mine a very good turn once."

MARGOT: "What sort of turn?"

PETER: "Sugar Candy insulted me at the Turf and I was knocking him into a jelly in Brick Street, when Wood intervened and saved his life. I can assure you he would do anything in the world for me and I'll make it all right! He shall have a handsome present."

MARGOT: "How vulgar! Having a brawl in Brick Street! How did you come to be in the East-end?"

PETER: "East-end! Why, it's next to Down Street, out of Piccadilly."

MARGOT: "It's very wrong to bribe the police, Peter!"

PETER: "I'm not going to bribe him, governess! I'm going to give him my Airedale terrier."

MARGOT: "What! That brute that killed the lady's lap-dog?"

PETER: "The very same!"

MARGOT: "God help poor Wood!"

Peter was so elated with this shattering escapade that a week after—on the occasion of another row, in which I pointed out that he was the most selfish man in the world—I heard him whistling under my bedroom window at midnight. Afraid lest he should wake my parents, I ran down in my dressing-gown to open the front door, but nothing would induce the chain to move. It was a newly acquired habit of the servants, started by Henry Hill from the night he had barred out the police. Being a hopeless mechanic and particularly weak in my fingers, I gave it up and went to the open window in the library. I begged him to go away, as nothing would induce me to forgive him, and I told him that my papa had only just retired to bed.

Peter, unmoved, ordered me to take the flower-pots off the window-sill, or he would knock them down and make a horrible noise, which would wake the whole house. After I had refused to do this, he said he would very likely break his neck when he jumped, as clearing the pots would mean hitting his head against the window frame. Fearing an explosion of temper, I weakly removed the flower-pots and watched his acrobatic feat with delight.

We had not been talking on the sofa for more than five minutes when I heard a shuffle of feet outside the library-door. I got up with lightning rapidity and put out the two candles on the writing-table with the palms of my hands, returning noise-lessly to Peter's side on the sofa, where we sat in black darkness. The door opened and my father came in holding a bedroom candle in his hand; he proceeded to walk stealthily round the room, looking at his pictures. The sofa on which we were sitting was in the window and had nothing behind it but the curtains. He held his candle high and close to every picture in turn and, putting his head forward, scanned them with tenderness and love. I saw Peter's idiotic hat and stick under the Gainsborough and could not resist nudging him as "The Ladies Erne and Dillon" were slowly approached. A candle held near one's face is the most blinding of all things and, after inspecting the sloping shoulders and anæmic features of the Gainsborough ladies, my father, quietly humming to himself, returned to his bed.

. . . . . . .

Things did not always go so smoothly with us. One night Peter suggested that I should walk away with him from the ball and try an American trotter which had been lent to him by a friend. As it was a glorious night, I thought it might be rather fun, so we walked down Grosvenor Street into Park Lane; and there stood the buggy under a lamp. American trotters always appear to be misshapen;

[165]

they are like coloured prints that are not quite in drawing and have never attracted me.

After we had placed ourselves firmly in the rickety buggy, Peter said to the man as he took the reins:

"Let him go, please!"

And go he did, with a curious rapid, swaying waddle. There was no traffic and we turned into the Edgware Road towards Hendon at a great pace, but Peter was a bad driver and after a little time said his arms ached and he thought it was time the "damned" horse was made to stop.

"I'm told the only way to stop an American trotter," said he, "is to hit him over the head."

At this I took the whip out of the socket and threw it into the road.

Peter, maddened by my action, shoved the reins into my hands, saying he would jump out. I did not take the smallest notice of this threat, but slackened the reins, after which we went quite slowly. I need hardly say Peter did not jump out, but suggested with severity that we should go back and look for the whip.

This was the last thing I intended to do, so when we turned I leant back in my seat and tugged at the

[166]

trotter with all my might, and we flew home without uttering a single word.

I was an excellent driver, but that night had taxed all my powers and, when we pulled up at the corner of Grosvenor Square, I ached in every limb. We were not in the habit of arriving together at the front door; and after he had handed me down to the pavement I felt rather awkward: I had no desire to break the silence, but neither did I want to take away Peter's coat, which I was wearing, so I said tentatively:

"Shall I give you your covert-coat?"

PETER: "Don't be childish! How can you walk back to the front door in your ball-dress? If any one happened to be looking out of the window, what would they think?"

This was really more than I could bear. I wrenched off his coat and placing it firmly on his arm, said:

"Most people, if they are sensible, are sound asleep at this time of the night, but I thank you all the same for your consideration."

We turned testily away from each other and I walked home alone. When I reached our front door my father opened it and, seeing me in my white tulle dress, was beside himself with rage. He asked me if I would kindly explain what I was doing, walking in the streets in my ball-dress at two in the morning. I told him exactly what had happened and warned him soothingly never to buy an American trotter; he told me that my reputation was ruined, that his was also and that my behaviour would kill my mother; I put my arms round his neck, told him soothingly that I had not really enjoyed myself *at all* and promised him that I would never do it again. By this time my mother had come out of her bedroom and was leaning over the staircase in her dressing-gown. She said in a pleading voice:

"Pray do not agitate yourself, Charlie. You've done a very wrong action, Margot! You really ought to have more consideration for your father: no one knows how impressionable he is. . . . Please tell Mr. Flower that we do not approve of him at all! . . ."

MARGOT: "You are absolutely right, dear mamma, and that is exactly what I have said to him more than once. But you need not worry, for no one saw us. Let's go to bed, darling, I'm dog-tired!"

. . . . . . .

Peter was thoroughly inconsequent about money and a great gambler; he told me one day in sorrow that his only chance of economising was to sell his horses and go to India to shoot big game, incidentally escaping his creditors.

When Peter went to India I was very unhappy, but to please my people I told them I would say good-bye and not write to him for a year, a promise which was faithfully kept.

While he was away, a young man of rank and fortune fell in love with me out hunting. He never proposed, he only declared himself. I liked him particularly, but his attention sat lightly on me; this rather nettled him and he told me one day riding home in the dark, that he was sure I must be in love with somebody else. I said that it did not at all follow and that, if he were wise he would stop talking about love and go and buy himself some good horses for Leicestershire, where I was going in a week to hunt with Lord Manners. We were staying together at Cholmondeley Castle, in Cheshire, with my beloved friend, Winifred Cholmondeley,* then Lady Rocksavage.

My new young man took my advice and went up

*The Marchioness of Cholmondeley.

to London, promising he would lend me "two of the best that money could buy" to take to Melton, where he proposed shortly to follow me.

When he arrived at Tattersalls there were several studs of well-known horses being sold: Jack Trotter's, Sir William Eden's and Lord Lonsdale's. Among the latter was a famous hunter, called Jack Madden, which had once belonged to Peter Flower; and my friend determined he would buy it for me. Some one said to him:

"I don't advise you to buy that horse, as you won't be able to ride it!"

(The fellow who related this to me added, "As you know, Miss Tennant, this is the only certain way by which you can sell any horse.")

Another man said:

"I don't agree with you, the horse is all right; when it belonged to Flower I saw Miss Margot going like a bird on it. . . ."

MY FRIEND: "Did Miss Tennant ride Flower's horses?"

At this the other fellow said:

"Why, my dear man, where *have* you lived! . . ."

.   .   .   .   .   .   .

Some months after I had ridden Jack Madden

and my own horses over high Leicestershire, my friend came to see me and asked me to swear on my Bible oath that I would not give him away over a secret which he intended to tell me.

After I had taken my solemn oath he said:

"Your friend Peter Flower in India was going to be put in the bankruptcy court and turned out of every club in London; so I went to Sam Lewis and paid his debt, but I don't want him to know about it and he never need, unless you tell him."

MARGOT: "What does he owe? And whom does he owe it to?"

MY FRIEND: "He owes ten thousand pounds, but I'm not at liberty to tell you who it's to; he is a friend of mine and a very good fellow. I can assure you that he has waited longer than most people would for Flower to pay him and I think he's done the right thing."

MARGOT: "Is Peter Flower a friend of yours?"

MY FRIEND: "I don't know him by sight and have never spoken to him in my life, but he's the man you're in love with and that is enough for me."

.    .    .    .    .    .    .

When the year was up and Peter—for all I knew —was still in India, I had made up my mind that, come what might, I would never, under any circumstances, renew my relations with him.

That winter I was staying with the Manners, as usual, and finding myself late for a near meet cut across country. Larking is always a stupid thing to do; horses that have never put a foot wrong generally refuse the smallest fence and rather than upset them at the beginning of the day you end by going through the gate, which you had better have done at first.

I had a mare called Molly Bawn, given to me by my fiancé, who was the finest timber-jumper in Leicestershire, and, seeing the people at the meet watching me as I approached, I could not resist, out of pure swagger, jumping an enormous gate. I said to myself how disgusted Peter would have been at my vulgarity! But at the same time it put me in good spirits. Something, however, made me turn round; I saw a man behind me, jumping the fence beside my gate; and there was Peter Flower! He was in tearing spirits and told me with eagerness how completely he had turned over a new leaf and never intended doing this, that or the other again, as far the most wonderful thing had happened to him that ever happened to any one.

[172]

"I'm under a lucky star, Margie! By heavens I am! And the joy of seeing you is *so great* that I won't allude to the gate, or Molly Bawn, or you, or any thing ugly! Let us enjoy ourselves for once; and for God's sake don't scold me. Are you glad to see me? Let me look at you! Which do you love best, Molly Bawn or me? Don't answer but listen."

He then proceeded to tell me how his debts had been paid by Sam Lewis—the money-lender— through an unknown benefactor and how he had begged Lewis to tell who it was, but that he had refused, having taken his oath never to reveal the name. My heart beat and I said a remarkably stupid thing:

"How wonderful! But you'll have to pay him back, Peter, won't you?"

PETER: "Oh, indeed! Then perhaps you can tell me who it is. . . ."

MARGOT: "How can I?"

PETER: "Do you know who it is?"

MARGOT: "I do not."

I felt the cock ought to have crowed, but I said nothing; and Peter was so busy greeting his friends in the field that I prayed he had not observed my guilty face.

[173]

Some days after this there was a race meeting at Leicester. Lord Lonsdale took a special at Oakham for the occasion and the Manners, Peter and I all went to the races. When I walked into the paddock, I saw my new friend—the owner of Jack Madden—talking to the Prince of Wales. When we joined them, the Prince suggested that we should go and see Mrs. Langtry's horse start, as it was a great rogue and difficult to mount.

As we approached the Langtry horse, the crowd made way for us and I found my friend next to me; on his other side was Peter Flower and then the Prince. The horse had his eyes bandaged and one of his forelegs was being held by a stable-boy. When the jockey was up and the bandage removed, it jumped into the air and gave an extended and violent buck. I was standing so near that I felt the draught of its kick on my hair. At this my friend gave a slight scream and, putting his arm round me, pulled me back towards him. A miss is as good as a mile, so after thanking him for his protection I chatted cheerfully to the Prince of Wales.

There is nothing so tiring as racing and we all sat

in perfect silence going home in the special that evening.

Neither at dinner nor after had I any opportunity of speaking to Peter, but I observed a singularly impassive expression on his face. The next day—being Sunday—I asked him to go round the stables with me after church; he refused, so I went alone. After dinner I tried again to talk to him, but he would not answer; he did not look angry, but he appeared to be profoundly sad, which depressed me. He told Hoppy Manners he was not going to hunt that week as he feared he would have to be in London. My heart sank. We all went to our rooms early and Peter remained downstairs reading. As he never read in winter I knew there was something seriously wrong, so I went down in my tea-gown to see him. It was nearly midnight. The room was empty and we were alone. He never looked up.

MARGOT: "Peter, you've not spoken to me once since the races. What can have happened?"

PETER: "I would rather you left me, *please*. . . . Pray go back to your room."

MARGOT (*sitting on the sofa beside him*): "Won't you speak to me and tell me all about it?"

[175]

Peter put down his book, and looking at me steadily, said very slowly:

"I'd rather not speak to a liar!"

I stood up as if I had been shot and said:

"How dare you say such a thing!"

PETER: "You lied to me."

MARGOT: "When?"

PETER: "You know perfectly well! And you are in love! You know you are. Will you deny it?"

"Oh! it's this that worries you, is it?" said I sweetly. "What would you say if I told you I was *not?*"

PETER: "I would say you were lying again."

MARGOT: "Have I ever lied to you, Peter?"

PETER: "How can I tell? (*Shrugging his shoulders*) You have lied twice, so I presume since I've been away you've got into the habit of it."

MARGOT: "Peter!"

PETER: "A man doesn't scream and put his arm round a woman, as D——ly did at the races to-day, unless he is in love. Will you tell me who paid my debt, please?"

MARGOT: "No, I won't."

PETER: "Was it D——ly?"

[176]

FOUR GENERATIONS OF ENGLAND'S ROYAL FAMILY: QUEEN
VICTORIA, KING EDWARD VII, KING GEORGE V AND
HIS SON, THE PRINCE OF WALES

MARGOT: "I shan't tell you. I'm not Sam Lewis; and, since I'm such a liar, is it worth while asking me these stupid questions?"

PETER: "Ah, Margot, this is the worst blow of my life! I see you are deceiving me. I know who paid my debt now."

MARGOT: "Then why ask *me?* . . ."

PETER: "When I went to India I had never spoken to D——ly in my life. Why should he have paid my debts for me? You had much better tell me the simple truth and get it over: it's all settled and you're going to marry him."

MARGOT: "Since I've got into the way of lying, you might spare yourself and me these vulgar questions."

PETER (*seizing my hands in anguish*): "Say you aren't going to marry him . . . tell me, tell me it's *not* true."

MARGOT: "Why should I? He has never asked me to."

.    .    .    .    .    .    .

After this the question of matrimony was bound to come up between us. The first time it was talked of, I was filled with anxiety. It seemed to put a finish to the radiance of our friendship and, worse

[177]

than that, it brought me up against my father, who had often said to me:

"You will never marry Flower; you must marry your superior."

Peter himself, in a subconscious way, had become aware of the situation. One evening, riding home, he said:

"Margie, do you see that?"

He pointed to the spire of the Melton Church and added:

"That is what you are in my life. I am not worth the button on your boot!"

To which I replied:

"I would not say that, but I cannot find goodness for two."

I was profundly unhappy. To live for ever with a man who was incapable of loving any one but himself and me, who was without any kind of moral ambition and chronically indifferent to politics and religion, was a nightmare.

I said to him:

"I will marry you if you get some serious occupation, Peter, but I won't marry an idle man; you think of nothing but yourself and me."

[178]

PETER: "What in the name of goodness would you have me think of? Geography?"

MARGOT: "You know exactly what I mean. Your power lies in love-making, not in loving; you don't love any one but yourself."

At this, Peter moved away from me as if I had struck him and said in a low tense voice:

"I am glad I did not say that. I would not care to have said such a cat-cruel thing; but I pity the man who marries you! He will think—as I did—that you are impulsively, throbbingly warm and kind and gentle; and he will find that he has married a governess and a prig; and a woman whose fire—of which she boasts so much—blasts his soul."

I listened to a Peter I had never heard before, His face frightened me. It indicated suffering. I put my head against his and said:

"How can I make an honest man of you, my dearest?"

. . . . . . .

I was getting quite clever about people, as the Mrs. Bo episode had taught me a lot.

A short time after this conversation, I observed a dark, good-looking woman pursuing Peter Flower at every ball and party. He told me when

I teased him that she failed to arrest his attention and that, for the first time in my life, I flattered him by my jealousy. I persisted and said that I did not know if it was jealousy but that I was convinced she was a bad friend for him.

PETER: "I've always noticed you think things bad when they don't suit you, but why should I give up my life to you? What do you give me in return? I'm the laughing-stock of London! But, if it is any satisfaction to you, I well tell you I don't care for the black lady, as you call her, and I never see her except at parties."

I knew Peter as well as a cat knows its way in the dark and I felt the truth of his remark: what did I give him? But I was not in a humour to argue.

The lady often asked me to go and see her, but I shrank from it and had never been inside her house.

One day I told Peter I would meet him at the Soane Collection in Lincoln's Inn Fields. To my surprise he said he had engaged himself to see his sister, who had been ill, and pointed out with a laugh that my governessing was taking root. He added:

[180]

"I don't mind giving it up if you can spend the whole afternoon with me."

I told him I would not have him give up going to see his sister for the world.

Finding myself at a loose end, I thought I would pay a visit to the black lady, as it was unworthy of me to have such a prejudice against some one whom I did not know. It was a hot London day; pale colours, thin stuffs, naked throats and large hats were strewn about the parks and streets.

When I arrived, the lady's bell was answered by a hall-boy and, hearing the piano, I told him he need not announce me. When I opened the door, I saw Peter and the dark lady sharing the same seat in front of the open piano. She wore a black satin sleeveless tea-gown, cut low at the throat, with a coral ribbon round her waist, and she had stuck a white rose in her rather dishevelled Carmen hair. I stood still, startled by her beauty and stunned by Peter's face. She got up, charmed to see me, and expressed her joy at the amazing luck which had brought me there that very afternoon, as she had a wonderful Spaniàrd coming to play to her after tea and she had often been told by Peter how musical I was, etc., etc. She hoped I was not shocked by her appearance, but she has just come back from a studio and it was too hot to expect people to get into decent clothes. She was perfectly at her ease and more than welcoming; before I could answer, she rallied Peter and said she pleaded guilty of having lured him away from the path of duty that afternoon, ending with a slight twinkle:

"From what I'm told, Miss Margot, you would *never* have done anything so wicked? . . ."

I felt ice in my blood and said:

"You needn't believe that! I've lured him away from the path of duty for the last eight years, haven't I, Peter?"

There was an uncomfortable silence and I looked about for a means of escape, but it took me some little time to find one.

I said good-bye and left the house.

When I was alone I locked the door, flung myself on my sofa, and was blinded by tears. Peter was right; he had said, "Why should I give up my life to you?" Why indeed! And yet, after eight years, this seemed a terrible ending to me.

"What do you give me in return?" What indeed? What claim had I to his fidelity? I thought I was giving gold for silver, but the dark lady would have called it copper for gold. Was she prepared to give everything for nothing? Why should I call it nothing? What did I know of Peter's love for her? All I knew was she had taught him to lie; and he must love her very much to do that: he had never lied to me before.

I went to the opera that night with my father and mother. Peter came into our box in a state of intense misery; I could hardly look at him. He put his hand out toward me under the programme and I took it.

At that moment the servant brought me a note and asked me to give her the answer. I opened it and this was what I read:

"If you want to do a very kind thing come and see me after the opera to-night. Don't say no."

I showed it to Peter, and he said, "Go." It was from the dark lady; I asked him what she wanted me for and he said she was terribly unhappy.

"Ah, Peter," said I, "what *have* you done? . . ."

PETER: "I know . . . it's quite true; but I've broken it off for ever with her."

Nothing he could have said then would have lightened my heart.

I scribbled, "Yes," on the same paper and gave it back to the girl.

When I said good night to my mother that night after the opera, I told her where I was going. Peter was standing in the front hall and took me in a hansom to the lady's house, saying he would wait for me round the corner while I had my interview with her.

It was past midnight and I felt overpoweringly tired. My beautiful rival opened the front door to me and I followed her silently up to her bedroom. She took off my opera-cloak and we sat down facing each other. The room was large and dark but for a row of candles on the mantel-piece and two high church-lights each side of a silver pier-glass. There was a table near my chair with odds and ends on it and a general smell of scent and flowers. I looked at her in her blue satin night-gown and saw that she had been crying.

"It is kind of you to have come," she said, "and I daresay you know why I wanted to see you to-night."

MARGOT: "No, I don't; I haven't the faintest idea!"

THE LADY (*looking rather embarrassed, but after a moment's pause*): "I want you to tell me about yourself."

I felt this to be a wrong entry: she had sent for me to tell her about Peter Flower and not myself; but why should I tell her about either of us? I had never spoken of my love-affairs excepting to my mother and my three friends—Con Manners, Frances Horner, and Etty Desborough—and people had ceased speaking to me about them; why should I sit up with a stranger and discuss myself at this time of night? I said there was nothing to tell. She answered by saying she had met so many people who cared for me that she felt she almost knew me, to which I replied:

"In that case, why talk about me?"

THE LADY: "But some people care for both of us."

MARGOT (*rather coldly*): "I daresay."

THE LADY: "Don't be hard, I want to know if you love Peter Flower. . . . Do you intend to marry him?"

The question had come then: this terrible question which my mother had never asked and which I had

always evaded! Had it got to be answered now
. . . and to a stranger?

With a determined effort to control myself I
said:

"You mean, am I engaged to be married?"

THE LADY: "I mean what I say; are you going
to marry Peter?"

MARGOT: "I have never told him I would."

THE LADY (*very slowly*): "Remember, my life
is bound up in your answer. . . ."

Her words seemed to burn and I felt a kind of
pity for her. She was leaning forward with her
eyes fastened on mine and her hands clasped between her knees.

"If you don't love him enough to marry him,
why don't you leave him alone?" she said. "Why
do you keep him bound to you? Why don't you
set him free?"

MARGOT: "He is free to love whom he likes; I
don't keep him, but I won't share him."

THE LADY: "You don't love him, but you want
to keep him; that is pure selfishness and vanity."

MARGOT: "Not at all! I would give him up
to-morrow and have told him so a thousand times,

if he would marry; but he is not in a position to marry any one."

THE LADY: "How can you say such a thing! His debts have just been paid by God knows who—some woman, I suppose!—and you are rich yourself. What is there to hinder you from marrying him?"

MARGOT: "That was not what I was thinking about. I don't believe you would understand even if I were to explain it to you."

THE LADY: "If you were really in love you could not be so critical and censorious."

MARGOT: "Oh, yes, I could! You don't know me."

THE LADY: "I love him in a way you would never understand. There is nothing in the world I would not do for him! No pain I would not suffer and no sacrifice I would not make."

MARGOT: "What could you do for him that would help him?"

THE LADY: "I would leave my husband and my children and go right away with him."

I felt as if she had stabbed me.

"Leave your children! and your husband!" I said. "But how can ruining them and yourself help Peter Flower? I don't believe for a moment he would ever do anything so vile."

THE LADY: "You think he loves you too much to run away with me, do you?"

MARGOT (*with indignation*): "Perhaps I hope he cares too much for *you*."

THE LADY (*not listening and getting up excitedly*): "What do you know about love? I have had a hundred lovers, but Peter Flower is the only man I have ever really cared for; and my life is at an end if you will not give him up."

MARGOT: "There is no question of my giving him up; he is free, I tell you. . . ."

THE LADY: "I tell you he is not! He doesn't *consider* himself free, he said as much to me this afternoon . . . when he wanted to break it all off."

MARGOT: "What do you wish me to do then? . . ."

THE LADY: "Tell Peter you don't love him in the right way, that you don't intend to marry him; and then leave him alone."

MARGOT: "Do you mean I am to leave him to you? . . . Do *you* love him in the right way?"

THE LADY: "Don't ask stupid questions. . . . I shall kill myself if he gives me up."

After this, I felt there was nothing more to be

said. I told her that Peter had a perfect right to do what he liked and that I had neither the will nor the power to influence his decision; that I was going abroad with my sister Lucy to Italy and would in any case not see him for several weeks; but I added that all my influence over him for years had been directed into making him the right sort of man to marry and that all hers would of necessity lie in the opposite direction. Not knowing quite how to say good-bye, I began to finger my cloak; seeing my intention, she said:

"Just wait one moment, will you? I want to know if you are as good as Peter always tells me you are; don't answer till I see your eyes. . . ."

She took two candles off the chimneypiece and placed them on the table near me, a little in front of my face, and then knelt upon the ground; I looked at her wonderful wild eyes and stretched out my hands towards her.

"Nonsense!" I said. "I am not in the least good! Get up! When I see you kneeling at my feet, I feel sorry for you."

THE LADY (*getting up abruptly*): "For God's sake don't pity me!"

. . . . . . .

[189]

Thinking over the situation in the calm of my room, I had no qualms as to either the elopement or the suicide, but I felt a revulsion of feeling towards Peter. His lack of moral indignation and purpose, his intractability in all that was serious and his incapacity to improve had been cutting a deep though unconscious division between us for years; and I determined at whatever cost, after this, that I would say good-bye to him.

A few days later, Lord Dufferin came to see me in Grosvenor Square.

"Margot," he said, "why don't you marry? You are twenty-seven; and life won't go on treating you so well if you go on treating it like this. As an old friend who loves you, let me give you one word of advice. You should marry in spite of being in love, but never because of it."

Before I went away to Italy, Peter and I, with passion-lit eyes and throbbing hearts, had said good-bye to each other for ever.

The relief of our friends at our parting was so suffocating that I clung to the shelter of my new friend, the stranger of that House of Commons dinner.

# CHAPTER V

MY husband's father was Joseph Dixon Asquith, a cloth-merchant, in Morley, at that time a small town outside Leeds. He was a man of high character who held Bible classes for young men. He married a daughter of William Willans, of Huddersfield, who sprang of an old Yorkshire Puritan stock.

He died when he was thirty-five, leaving four children: William Willans, Herbert Henry, Emily Evelyn and Lilian Josephine. They were brought up by their mother, who was a woman of genius. I named my only daughter* after Goethe's mother, but was glad when I found out that her grandmother Willans had been called Elizabeth.

*Princess Bibesco.

[191]

William Willans—who is dead—was the eldest of the family and a clever little man. He taught at Clifton College for over thirty years.

Lilian Josephine died when she was a baby; and Evelyn—one of the best of women—is the only near relation of my husband still living.

My husband's mother, old Mrs. Asquith, I never knew; my friend Mark Napier told me that she was a brilliantly clever woman but an invalid. She had delicate lungs, which obliged her to live on the South coast; and, when her two sons went to the City of London School, they lived alone together in lodgings in Islington and were both poor and industrious.

Although Henry's mother was an invalid she had a moral, religious and intellectual influence over her family that cannot be exaggerated. She was a profound reader and a brilliant talker and belonged to what was in those days called orthodox nonconformity, or Congregationalists.

After my husband's first marriage he made money by writing, lecturing and examining at Oxford. When he was called to the Bar success did not come to him at once.

He had no rich patron and no one to push him

HERBERT HENRY ASQUITH AS HE WAS WHEN HE RESIGNED THE
PREMIERSHIP TO LLOYD-GEORGE DURING THE WAR

RAYMOND ASQUITH, SON OF
HERBERT HENRY ASQUITH BY
HIS FIRST MARRIAGE. HE
WAS KILLED IN BELGIUM
DURING THE WAR

forward. He had made for himself a great Oxford reputation: he was a fine scholar and lawyer, but socially was not known by many people.

It was said that Gladstone only promoted men by seniority and never before knowing with precision what they were like, but in my husband's case it was not so.

Lord James of Hereford, then Sir Henry James, was Attorney General, overburdened with a large private practice at the Bar; and, when the great Bradlaugh case came on, in 1883, it was suggested to him that a young man living on the same staircase might devil the Affirmation Bill for him. This was the beginning of Asquith's career. When Gladstone saw the brief for his speech, he noted the fine handwriting and asked who had written it. Sir Henry James, the kindest and most generous of men, was delighted at Gladstone's observation and brought the young man to him. From that moment both the Attorney General and the Prime Minister marked him out for distinction; he rose without any intermediary step of an under-secretaryship from a back-bencher to a Cabinet Minister; and when we married in 1894 he was Home Secretary. In 1890 I cut and kept out of some newspapers this prophecy, little thinking that I would marry one of the "New English Party."

## A New English Party

Amid all the worry and turmoil and ambition of Irish politics, there is steadily growing up a little English party, of which more will be heard in the days that are to come. This is a band of philosophico-social Radicals—not the *old* type of *laissez-faire* politician, but quite otherwise. In other words, what I may call practical Socialism has caught on afresh with a knot of clever, youngish members of Parliament who sit below the gangway on the Radical side. This little group includes clever, learned, metaphysical Mr. Haldane, one of the rising lawyers of his day; young Sir Edward Grey, sincere, enthusiastic, with a certain gift for oratory, and helped by a beautiful and clever wife; Mr. Sidney Buxton, who has perhaps the most distinct genius for practical work; and finally, though in rather loose attachment to the rest, Mr. Asquith, brilliant, cynical, cold, clear, but with his eye on the future. The dominant ideas of this little band tend in the direction of moderate Collectivism—i.e., of municipal Socialism.

I met my husband for the first time in 1891, at a dinner given by Peter Flower's brother Cyril.* I had never heard of him in my life, which gives some indication of how I was wasting my time on two

*The late Lord Battersea.

worlds: I do not mean this and the next, but the sporting and dramatic, Melton in the winter and the Lyceum in the summer. My Coquelin coachings and my dancing-lessons had led me to rehearsals both of the ballet and the drama; and for a short time I was at the feet of Ellen Terry and Irving. I say "short" advisedly, for then as now I found Bohemian society duller than any English watering-place. Every one has a different conception of Hell and few of us connect it with flames; but stage suppers are my idea of Hell and, with the exception of Irving and Coquelin, Ellen Terry and Sarah Bernhardt, I have never met the hero or heroine off the stage that was not ultimately dull.

The dinner where I was introduced to Henry was in the House of Commons and I sat next to him. I was tremendously impressed by his conversation and his clean Cromwellian face. He was different from the others and, although abominably dressed, had so much personality that I made up my mind at once that here was a man who could help me and would understand everything. It never crossed my brain that he was married, nor would that have mattered; I had always been more anxious that Peter Flower should marry than myself, because he was thirteen years older than I was, but matrimony was not the austere purpose of either of our lives.

After dinner we all walked on the Terrace and I was flattered to find my new friend by my side. Lord Battersea chaffed me in his noisy, flamboyant manner, trying to separate us; but with tact and determination this frontal attack was resisted and my new friend and I retired to the darkest part of the Terrace, where, leaning over the parapet, we gazed into the river and talked far into the night.

Our host and his party—thinking that I had gone home and that Mr. Asquith had returned to the House when the division bell rang—had disappeared; and when we finished our conversation the Terrace was deserted and the sky light.

We met a few days later dining with Sir Algernon West—a very dear and early friend of mine—and after this we saw each other constantly. I found out from something he said to me that he was married and lived at Hampstead and that his days were divided between 1 Paper Buildings and the House of Commons. He told me that he had always been a shy man and in some ways this is true of him even now; but I am glad that I did not observe it at the time, as shy people disconcerted me: I liked modesty, I pitied timidity, but I was embarrassed by shyness.

I cannot truly say, however, that the word shy described my husband at any time: he was a little *gauche* in movement and blushed when he was praised, but I have never seen him nervous with any one or embarrassed by any social dilemma. His unerring instinct into all sorts of people and affairs —quite apart from his intellectual temperament and learning—and his incredible lack of vanity struck me at once. The art of making every man better pleased with himself he had in a high degree; and he retains to this day an incurable modesty.

When I discovered that he was married, I asked him to bring his wife to dinner, which he did, and directy I saw her I said:

"I do hope, Mrs. Asquith, you have not minded your husband dining here without you, but I rather gathered Hampstead was too far away for him to get back to you from the House of Commons. You must always let me know and come with him whenever it suits you."

. . . . . . .

In making this profound and attaching friendship with the stranger of that House of Commons dinner, I had placed myself in a difficult position when Helen Asquith died. To be a stepwife and a stepmother was unthinkable, but at the same time the moment had arrived when a decision—involving a great change in my life—had become inevitable. I had written to Peter Flower before we parted every day for nine years—with the exception of the months he had spent flying from his creditors in India—and I had prayed for him every night, but it had not brought more than happiness to both of us; and when I deliberately said good-bye to him I shut down a page of my life which, even if I had wished to, I could never have reopened. When Henry told me he cared for me, that unstifled inner voice which we all of us hear more or less indistinctly told me I would be untrue to myself and quite unworthy of life if, when such a man came knocking at the door, I did not fling it wide open.

The rumour that we were engaged to be married caused alarm amounting to consternation in certain circles. Both Lord Rosebery and Lord Randolph Churchill, without impugning me in any way, deplored the marriage, nor were they by any means alone in thinking such a union might ruin the life

of a promising politician. Some of my own friends
were equally apprehensive from another point of
view; to start my new life charged with a ready-
made family of children brought up very differently from myself, with a man who played no games
and cared for no sport, in London instead of in the
country, with no money except what he could make
at the Bar, was, they thought, taking too many
risks.

My Melton friends said it was a terrible waste
that I was not marrying a sporting man and told
me afterwards that they nearly signed a round-
robin to implore me never to give up hunting, but
feared I might think it impertinent.

The rumour of my engagement caused a sensation in the East-end of London as well as the West.
The following was posted to me by an anonymous
well-wisher:

At the meeting of the "unemployed" held on
Tower Hill yesterday afternoon, John E. Williams,
the organiser appointed by the Social Democratic
Federation, said that on the previous day they had
gone through the West-end squares and had let
the "loafers" living there know that they were alive.
On the previous evening he had seen an announcement which, at first sight, had caused tears to run

down his face, for he had thought it read, "Mr.
Asquith going to be murdered." However, it
turned out that Mr. Asquith was going to be married, and he accordingly proposed that the unemployed, following the example of the people in the
West-end, should forward the right hon. gentleman a congratulatory message. He moved: "That
this mass meeting of the unemployed held on Tower
Hill, hearing that Mr. Asquith is about to enter the
holy bonds of matrimony, and knowing he has no
sympathy for the unemployed, and that he has
lately used his position in the House of Commons
to insult the unemployed, trusts that his partner
will be one of the worst tartars it is possible for a
man to have, and that his family troubles will compel him to retire from political life, for which he is
so unfit." The reading of the resolution was followed by loud laughter and cheers. Mr. Crouch
(National Union of Boot and Shoe Operatives)
seconded the motion, which was supported by a
large number of other speakers and adopted.

I was much more afraid of spoiling Henry's life
than my own, and what with old ties and bothers,
and new ties and stepchildren, I deliberated a long
time before the final fixing of my wedding-day.

I had never met any of his children except little
Violet when I became engaged and he only took
me to see them once before we were married, as
they lived in a villa at Redhill under the charge of a

**Mr. Asquith and His Fiancée.**

Rarely has any social event, says a despatch by the HERALD'S Special Wire, created such widespread interest as the announcement of the engagement of Mr. Asquith to Miss Margot Tennant, and congratulations are general and sincere. Probably no young unmarried woman has ever before won for herself so remarkable a position as Miss Tennant has won in the heart of an unusually brilliant and competitive society. The circle in which she has been a leading spirit has been a subject of speculation, envy and misunderstanding, under their ridiculous name of "Souls," for some years past, but if they have not escaped from the unfortunate and inevitable disadvantage of a clique, they have at the same time quickened and stimulated a genuine if somewhat dilettante interest in things of mind as opposed to the ordinary frivolous interests of the hour, and for this they will be and deserve to be remembered.

THE FIANCÉ.

ANNOUNCEMENT IN "THE NEW YORK HERALD" FEBRUARY 1894 OF THE ENGAGEMENT OF MARGOT TENNANT AND HERBERT HENRY ASQUITH

kind and careful governess; he never spoke of
them except one day when, after my asking him if
he thought they would hate me and cataloguing my
grave imperfections and moderate qualifications for
the part, he stopped me and said that his eldest son,
Raymond, was remarkably clever and would be
devoted to me, adding thoughtfully:

"I think—and hope—he is ambitious."

This was a new idea to me: we had always been
told what a wicked thing ambition was; but we were
a fighting family of high spirits and not temper,
so we had acquiesced, without conforming to the
nursery dictum. The remark profoundly impressed me and I pondered it over in my heart. I
do not think, by the way, that it turned out to be a
true prophecy, but Raymond Asquith had such unusual intellectual gifts that no one could have con-
victed him of lack of ambition. To win without
work, to score without an effort and to delight without premeditation is given to few.

One night after our engagement we were dining
with Sir Henry and Lady Campbell-Bannerman.
While the women were talking and the men drink-
ing, dear old Mrs. Gladstone and other elderly
ladies and political wives took me on as to the duties

of the spouse of a possible Prime Minister; they were so eloquent and severe that at the end of it my nerves were racing round like a squirrel in a cage.

When Mr. Gladstone came into the drawing-room I felt depressed and, clinging to his arm, I switched him into a corner and said I feared the ladies took me for a jockey or a ballet-girl, as I had been adjured to give up, among other things, dancing, riding and acting. He patted my hand, said he knew no one better fitted to be the wife of a great politician than myself and ended by saying that, while I was entitled to discard exaggeration in rebuke, it was a great mistake not to take criticism wisely and in a spirit which might turn it to good account.

I have often thought of this when I see how brittle and egotistical people are at the smallest disapprobation. I never get over my surprise, old as I am, at the surly moral manners, the lack of humbleness and the colossal personal vanity that are the bed-rock of people's incapacity to take criticism well. There is no greater test of size than this; but, judged by this test, most of us are dwarfs.

·  ·  ·  ·  ·  ·  ·  ·  ·

Disapproving of long engagements and wishing to escape the cataract of advice by which my friends thought to secure both my husband's and my own matrimonial bliss, I hurried on my marriage. My friends and advisers made me unhappy at this time, but fortunately for me Henry Asquith is a compelling person and, in spite of the anxiety of the friends and relations, we were married at St. George's, Hanover Square, on May the 10th, 1894. I doubt if any bride ever received so many strange letters as I did. There was one which I kept in front of me when I felt discouraged. I shall not say who it is from, as the writer is alive:

My dear Margot,

You are not different to other people except in this respect—you have a clear, cold head, and a hot, keen heart, and you won't find *everything;* so choose what lasts, and with luck and with pluck, marrying as you are from the highest motives, you will be repaid. Asquith is far too good for you. He is not conventional, and will give you a great deal of freedom. He worships you, and understands you, and is bent on making the best of you and the life together. You are marrying a very uncommon man—not so much intellectually—but he is uncommon from his Determination, Reality and concentrated power of love. Don't pity yourself—you would not wish to have loved Peter less—

though you might wish you had never seen him—
but you must know you have allowed *too* much love
in your life, and must bear the consequences. Deep
down in your heart you must feel that you ought
to put a stop to your present life, and to the temptation of making people love you. Depend upon it
with your rich and warm nature you need not be
afraid of not loving Asquith intensely. By marrying him you will prove yourself to be a woman of
courage and nobility, instead of a woman who is
talked about and who is in reality self-indulgent.
You are lucky after your rather dangerous life to
have found such a haven and should bless God
for it.

In those days it was less common for people to
collect in the streets to see a wedding. The first
marriage I ever saw which collected a crowd was
Lady Crewe's, but her father, Lord Rosebery, was
a Derby winner and Prime Minister and she was
married in Westminster Abbey. From Grosvenor
Square to St. George's, Hanover Square, is a short
distance, but from our front door to the church the
pavements were blocked with excited and enthusiastic people.

An old nurse of my sister Charlotte's, Jerusha
Taylor, told me that a gentleman outside St.
George's had said to her, "I will give you £10 for
that ticket of yours!" and when she refused he said,

"I will give you *anything you like!* I must see Margot Tennant married!" I asked her what sort of a man he was. She answered,

"Oh! he was a real gentleman, ma'am! I know a gentleman when I see him; he had a gardenia in his buttonhole, but he didn't get my ticket!"

Our register was signed by four Prime Ministers: Mr. Gladstone, Lord Rosebery, Arthur Balfour and my husband. We spent the first part of our honeymoon at Mells Park, Frome, lent to us by Sir John and Lady Horner, and the second at Clovelly Court with our friend and hostess, Mrs. Hamlyn.

# CHAPTER VI

THE ASQUITH CHILDREN BY THE FIRST MARRIAGE—
MARGOT'S STEPDAUGHTER VIOLET—MEMORY OF
THE FIRST MRS. ASQUITH—RAYMOND'S BRIL-
LIANT CAREER—ARTHUR'S HEROISM IN THE
WAR

I DO not think if you had ransacked the world
you could have found natures so opposite in
temper, temperament and outlook as myself and my
stepchildren when I first knew them.

If there was a difference between the Tennants
and Lytteltons of laughter, there was a difference
between the Tennants and Asquiths of tears. Tennants believed in appealing to the hearts of men,
firing their imagination and penetrating and vivify-
ing their inmost lives. They had a little loose love
to give the whole world. The Asquiths—without
mental flurry and with perfect self-mastery—believed in the free application of intellect to every
human emotion; no event could have given height-
ened expression to their feelings. Shy, self-en-
gaged, critical and controversial, nothing surprised

[208]

them and nothing upset them. We were as zealous and vital as they were detached and as cocky and passionate as they were modest and emotionless.

They rarely looked at you and never got up when any one came into the room. If you had appeared downstairs in a ball-dress or a bathing-gown they would not have observed it and would certainly never have commented upon it if they had. Whether they were glowing with joy at the sight of you or thrilled at receiving a friend, their welcome was equally composed. They were devoted to one another and never quarrelled; they were seldom wild and never naughty. Perfectly self-contained, truthful and deliberate, I never saw them lose themselves in my life and I have hardly ever seen the saint or hero that excited their disinterested emotion.

When I thought of the storms of revolt, the rage, the despair, the wild enthusiasms and reckless adventures, the disputes that finished not merely with fights, but with fists in our nursery and schoolroom, I was stunned by the steadiness of the Asquith temper.

Let it not be inferred that I am criticising them as they now are, or that their attitude towards myself was at any time lacking in sympathy. Blindness of heart does not imply hardness; and expression is a matter of temperament or impulse; but it was their attitude towards life that was different from my own. They over-valued brains, which was a strange fault, as they were all remarkably clever.

Hardly any Prime Minister has had famous children, but the Asquiths were all conspicuous in their different ways: Raymond and Violet the most striking, Arthur the most capable, Herbert a poet and Cyril the shyest and the rarest.

. . . . . . .

Cys Asquith, who was the youngest of the family, combined what was best in all of them morally and intellectually and possessed what was finer than brains.

He was two, when his mother died, and a clumsy ugly little boy with a certain amount of graceless obstinacy, with which both Tennants and Asquiths were equally endowed. To the casual observer he would have appeared less like me than any of my step-family, but as a matter of fact he and I had the most in common; we shared a certain spiritual foundation and moral aspiration that solder people together through life.

# AN AUTOBIOGRAPHY

It is not because I took charge of him at an early age that I say he is more my own than the others, but because, although he did not always agree with me, he never misunderstood me. He said at Mürren one day, when he was seventeen and we had been talking together on life and religion:

"It must be curious for you, Margot, seeing all of us laughing at things that make you cry."

This showed remarkable insight for a schoolboy. When I look at his wonderful face now and think of his appearance at the time of our marriage, I am reminded of the Hans Andersen toad with the jewel in its head, but the toad is no longer there.

I have a dear friend called Bogie Harris,* who told me that, at a ball given by Con and Hoppy Manners, he had seen a young man whose face had struck him so much that he looked about for some one in the room to tell him who it was. That young man was Cyril Asquith.

One night when he was a little boy, after I had heard him say his prayers he asked me to read the General Confession out of his Prayer Book to him. It was such an unusual request that I said:

"Very well, darling, I will, but first of all I must

*Mr. H. Harris, of Bedford Square.

[211]

read you what I love best in the Prayer Book."

To which he answered:

"Oh, do! I should like that."

I put a cushion behind my head and, lying down beside him, read:

"Lighten our darkness, we beseech Thee, O Lord; and by Thy great mercy defend us from all perils and dangers of this night, for the love of Thine only Son, our Saviour Jesus Christ. Amen."

After this I read him the General Confession, opening, "We have erred and strayed from Thy ways like lost sheep," and ending, "that we may hereafter live a godly, righteous, and sober life." When I had finished I said to him:

"What do you take sober to mean here, darling?"

Cys (*looking furtively at me with his little green eyes*): "It does not mean drunkenness." (*A slight pause; then reflectively*): "I should say moderate living."

I told the children one day to collect some of their toys and that I would take them to the hospital, where they could give them away themselves. I purposely did not say broken toys; and a few days afterwards I was invited to the nursery. On arriving upstairs I saw that Cys's eyes were scarlet; and set out in pathetic array round the room was a large family of monkeys christened by him "the Thumblekins." They were what he loved best in the world. I observed that they were the only unbroken toys that were brought to me; and he was eyeing his treasures with anguish in his soul. I was so touched that I could hardly speak; and, when I put my arms round his neck, he burst into sobs:

"May I keep one monkey . . . only one, Margot? . . . *Please?* . . . *Please,* Margot? . . ."

This was the window in his soul that has never been closed to me. For many years during a distinguished college career he was delicate, but since his marriage to Miss Ann Pollock—a daylight creature of charm, beauty and goodness—he has been happy and strong.

.    .    .    .    .    .    .

My stepdaughter Violet—now Lady Bonham Carter—though intensely feminine, would have made a remarkable man. I do not believe there is any examination she could not have passed either at a public school or a university. Born without shyness or trepidation, from her youth upwards she had perfect self-possession and patience. She loved dialectics and could put her case logically, plausibly and eloquently; and, although quite as unemotional as her brothers, she had more enterprise and indignation. In her youth she was delicate, and what the French call *très personelle;* and this prevented her going through the mill of rivalry and criticism which had been the daily bread of my girlhood.

She had the same penetrating sense of humour as her brother Raymond and quite as much presence of mind in retort. Her gift of expression was amazing and her memory unrivalled. My daughter Elizabeth and she were the only girls except myself that I ever met who were real politicians, not interested merely in the personal side—whether Mr. B. or C. spoke well or was likely to get promoted—but in the legislation and administration of Parliament; they followed and knew what was going on at home and abroad and enjoyed friendships with most of the young and famous men of the day. Violet Bonham Carter has, I think, a great political future in the country if not in the Commons. She is a natural speaker, easy, eloquent, witty, short and of imperturbable *sang-froid.*

Life in the House is neither healthy, useful nor appropriate for a woman; and the functions of a mother and a member of Parliament are not compatible. This was one of the reasons why my husband and I were against giving the franchise to women. Violet is a real mother and feels the problem acutely, but she is a real Liberal also and, with gifts as conspicuous as hers, she must inevitably exercise a wide-spread political influence. Her speeches in her father's election at Paisley, in February of this year, brought her before a general as well as intellectual audience from which she can never retire; and, whenever she appears on a platform, the public shout from every part of the hall calling on her to speak.

· · · · · · ·

Raymond Asquith was born on the 6th of November, 1878, and was killed fighting against the Germans before his regiment had been in action ten minutes, on the 15th of September, 1916.

He was intellectually one of the most distinguished young men of his day and beautiful to look at, added to which he was light in hand, brilliant in answer and interested in affairs. When he went to Balliol he cultivated a kind of cynicism which was an endless source of delight to the young people around him; in a good-humoured way he made a butt of God and smiled at man. If he had been really keen about any one thing—law or literature —he would have made the world ring with his name, but he lacked temperament and a certain sort of imagination and was without ambition of any kind.

His education was started by a woman in a day-school at Hampstead; from there he took a Winchester scholarship and he became a scholar of Balliol. At Oxford he went from triumph to triumph. He took a first in classical moderations in 1899; first-class *literæ humaniores* in 1901; first-class jurisprudence in 1902. He won the Craven, Ireland, Derby and Eldon scholarships. He was President of the Union and became a Fellow of All Souls in 1902; and after he left Oxford he was called to the Bar in 1904.

In spite of this record, a more modest fellow about his own achievements never lived.

Raymond was charming and good-tempered from his boyhood and I only remember him once in his life getting angry with me. He had been urged to go into politics by both his wife and his father and had been invited by the Liberal Association of a northern town to become their candidate. He was complaining about it one day to me, saying how dull, how stupid, how boring the average constituents of all electorates were; I told him I thought a closer contact with common people would turn out not only more interesting and delightful than he imagined, but that it would be the making of him. He flared up at once and made me appear infinitely ridiculous, but being on sure ground I listened with amusement and indifference; the discussion ended amicably, neither of us having deviated by a hair's breath from our original positions. He and I seldom got on each other's nerves, though two more different beings never lived. His arctic analysis of what he looked upon as "cant" always stirred his listeners to a high pitch of enthusiasm.

One day when he was at home for his holidays and we were all having tea together, to amuse the children I began asking riddles. I told them that I had only guessed one in my life, but it had taken me three days. They asked me what it was, and I said:

"What is it that God has never seen, that kings see seldom and that we see every day?"

Raymond instantly answered:

"A joke."

I felt that the real answer, which was "an equal," was very tepid after this.

In 1907 he married, from 10 Downing Street, Katherine Horner, a beautiful creature of character and intellect, as lacking in fire and incense as himself. Their devotion to each other and happiness was a perpetual joy to me, as I felt that in some ways I had contributed to it. Katherine was the daughter of Laura's greatest friend, Frances Horner, and he met her through me.

Raymond found in both his mother-in-law and Sir John Horner friends capable of appreciating his fine flavour. He wrote with ease and brilliance both prose and poetry. I will quote two of his poems:

### In Praise of Young Girls

Attend my Muse, and, if you can, approve
While I proclaim the "speeding up" of Love;
For Love and Commerce hold a common creed—
The scale of business varies with the speed;
For Queen of Beauty or for Sausage King
The customer is always on the wing—
Then praise the nymph who regularly earns
Small profits (if you please) but quick returns.
Our modish Venus is a bustling minx,
But who can spare the time to woo a sphinx?
When Mona Lisa posed with rustic guile

# AN AUTOBIOGRAPHY

The stale enigma of her simple smile,
Her leisure lovers raised a pious cheer
While the slow mischief crept from ear to ear.
Poor listless Lombard, you would ne'er engage
The brisker beaux of our mercurial age
Whose lively mettle can as easy brook
An epic poem as a lingering look—
Our modern maiden smears the twig with lime
For twice as many hearts in half the time.
Long ere the circle of that staid grimace
Has wheeled your weary dimples into place,
Our little Chloe (mark the nimble fiend!)
Has raised a laugh against her bosom friend,
Melted a marquis, mollified a Jew,
Kissed every member of the Eton crew,
Ogled a Bishop, quizzed an aged peer,
Has danced a Tango and has dropped a tear.
Fresh from the schoolroom, pink and plump and
      pert,
Bedizened, bouncing, artful and alert,
No victim she of vapours and of moods
Though the sky falls she's "ready with the goods"..
Polite or gothic, libertine or chaste,
Supply a waspish tongue, a waspish waist,
Astarte's breast or Atalanta's leg,
Love ready-made, or glamour off the peg—
Do you prefer: "a thing of dew and air"?
Or is your type Poppæa or Polaire?
The crystal casket of a maiden's dreams,
Or the last fancy in cosmetic creams?
The dark and tender or the fierce and bright,
Youth's rosy blush or Passion's pearly bite?
You hardly know perhaps; but Chloe knows,

# MARGOT ASQUITH

And pours you out the necessary dose,
Meticulously measuring to scale
The cup of Circe or the Holy Grail—
An actress she at home in every rôle,
Can flout or flatter, bully or cajole,
And on occasion by a stretch of art
Can even speak the language of the heart,
Can lisp and sigh and make confused replies,
With baby lips and complicated eyes,
Indifferently apt to weep or wink,
Primly pursue, provocatively shrink,
Brazen or bashful, as the case require,
Coax the faint baron, curb the bold esquire,
Deride restraint, but deprecate desire,
Unbridled yet unloving, loose but limp,
Voluptuary, virgin, prude and pimp.

LINES TO A YOUNG VISCOUNT, WHO DIED AT OX-
FORD, ON THE MORROW OF A BUMP SUPPER (*by the
President of his College*)

Dear Viscount, in whose ancient blood
    The blueness of the bird of March,
    The vermeil of the tufted larch,
Are fused in one magenta flood.

Dear Viscount—ah! to me how dear,
    Who even in thy frolic mood
    Discerned (or sometimes thought I could)
The pure proud purpose of a peer!

So on the last sad night of all
    Erect among the reeling rout

# AN AUTOBIOGRAPHY

You beat your tangled music out
Lofty, aloof, viscontial.

You struck a bootbath with a can,
    And with the can you struck the bath,
    There on the yellow gravel path,
As gentleman to gentleman.

We met, we stood, we faced, we talked
    While those of baser birth withdrew;
    I told you of an Earl I knew;
You said you thought the wine was corked;

And so we parted—on my lips
    A light farewell, but in my soul
    The image of a perfect whole,
A Viscount to the finger tips——

An image—Yes; but thou art gone;
    For nature red in tooth and claw
    Subsumes under an equal law
Viscount and Iguanodon.

Yet we who know the Larger Love,
    Which separates the sheep and goats
    And segregates Scolecobrots,*
Believing where we cannot prove,

Deem that in His mysterious Day
    God puts the Peers upon His right,
    And hides the poor in endless night,
For thou, my Lord, art more than they.

*A word from the Greek Testament meaning people who are eaten
by worms.

It is a commonplace to say after a man is dead that he could have done anything he liked in life: it is nearly always exaggerated; but of Raymond Asquith the phrase would have been true.

His oldest friend was Harold Baker,* a man whose academic career was as fine as his own and whose changeless affection and intimacy we have long valued; but Raymond had many friends as well as admirers. His death was the first great sorrow in my stepchildren's lives and an anguish to his father and me. The news of it came as a terrible shock to every one. My husband's natural pride and interest in him had always been intense and we were never tired of discussing him when we were alone: his personal charm and wit, his little faults and above all the success which so certainly awaited him. Henry's grief darkened the waters in Downing Street at a time when, had they been clear, certain events could never have taken place.

When Raymond was dying on the battle-field he gave the doctor his flask to give to his father; it was placed by the side of his bed and never moved till we left Whitehall.

I had not realised before how powerless a step-

*The Rt. Hon. Harold Baker.

wife is when her husband is mourning the death of his child; and not for the first time I profoundly wished that Raymond had been my son.

Among the many letters we received, this one from Sir Edward Grey, the present Lord Grey of Fallodon, gave my husband the most comfort:

33 ECCLESTON SQUARE,
S.W.
*Sept.* 18, 1916.

MY DEAR ASQUITH,

A generation has passed since Raymond's mother died and the years that have gone make me feel for and with you even more than I would then. Raymond has had a brilliant and unblemished life; he chose with courage the heroic part in this war and he has died as a hero.

If this life be all, it matters not whether its years be few or many, but if it be not all, then Raymond's life is part of something that is not made less by his death, but is made greater and ennobled by the quality and merit of his life and death.

I would fain believe that those who die do not suffer in the separation from those they love here; that time is not to them what it is to us, and that to them the years of separation be they few or many will be but as yesterday.

If so then only for us, who are left here, is the pain of suffering and the weariness of waiting and

[223]

enduring; the one beloved is spared that. There is some comfort in thinking that it is we, not the loved one, that have the harder part.

I grieve especially for Raymond's wife, whose suffering I fear must be what is unbearable. I hope the knowledge of how the feelings of your friends and the whole nation, and not of this nation only, for you is quickened and goes out to you will help you to continue the public work, which is now more than ever necessary, and will give you strength. Your courage I know never fails.

Yours affectionately,

EDWARD GREY.

Raymond Asquith was the bravest of the brave, nor did he ever complain of anything that fell to his lot while he was soldiering.

It might have been written of him:

> He died
> As one that had been studied in his death
> To throw away the dearest thing he own'd.
> As 'twere a careless trifle.

—*Macbeth, Act I., sc. iv.*

. . . . . . .

Our second son, Herbert, began his career as a lawyer. He had a sweet and gentle nature and much originality. He was a poet and wrote the following some years before the Great War of

PRINCESS BIBESCO, MARGOT ASQUITH'S ONLY DAUGHTER, WHO
MARRIED PRINCE BIBESCO, RUMANIAN DIPLOMAT

# AN AUTOBIOGRAPHY

1914, through which he served from the first day
to the last:

## THE VOLUNTEER*

Here lies a clerk who half his life had spent
Toiling at ledgers in a city grey,
Thinking that so his days would drift away
With no lance broken in life's tournament;
Yet ever 'twixt the book and his bright eyes
The gleaming eagles of the legions came,
And horsemen, charging under phantom skies,
Went thundering past beneath the oriflamme.

And now those waiting dreams are satisfied,
From twilight to the halls of dawn he went;
His lance is broken—but he lies content
With that high hour, he wants no recompense,
Who found his battle in the last resort,
Nor needs he any hearse to bear him hence,
Who goes to join the men at Agincourt.

He wrote this when he was in Flanders in the
war:

## THE FALLEN SPIRE*
### (A Flemish Village)

That spire is gone that slept for centuries,
    Mirrored among the lilies, calm and low;
And now the water holds but empty skies
    Through which the rivers of the thunder flow.

*Reprinted from *The Volunteer and other Poems,* by kind permission of Messrs. Sidgwick & Jackson.

The church lies broken near the fallen spire,
    For here, among these old and human things,
Death sweeps along the street with feet of fire,
    And goes upon his way with moaning wings.

On pavements by the kneeling herdsmen worn
    The drifting fleeces of the shells are rolled;
Above the Saints a village Christ forlorn,
    Wounded again, looks down upon His fold.

And silence follows fast: no evening peace,
    But leaden stillness, when the thunder wanes,
Haunting the slender branches of the trees,
    And settling low upon the listless plains.

"Beb," as we called him, married Lady Cynthia Charteris, a lovely niece of Lady de Vesci and daughter of another beloved and interesting friend of mine, the present Countess of Wemyss.

Our third son, Arthur Asquith, was one of the great soldiers of the war. He married Betty, the daughter of my greatest friend, Lady Manners, a woman who has never failed me in affection and loyalty.

Arthur Asquith joined the Royal Naval Division on its formation in September, 1914, and was attached at first to the "Anson," and during the greater part of his service to the "Hood" Battalion.

In the early days of October, 1914, he took part in the operations at Antwerp and, after further training at home in the camp at Blandford, went in February, 1915, with his battalion to the Dardanelles, where they formed part of the Second Naval Brigade. He was in all the fighting on the Gallipoli peninsula and was wounded, but returned to duty and was one of the last to embark on the final evacuation of Helles, in January, 1916.

In the following May the Naval Division joined the army in France, becoming the 63rd Division, and the "Hood" Battalion (now commanded by Commander Freyberg, V. C.) formed part of the 189th Brigade.

In the Battle of the Ancre (February, 1917) Arthur Asquith was severely wounded and was awarded the D.S.O.

In the following April, Commander Freyberg having been promoted to be a Brigadier, Arthur Asquith took over the command of the "Hood" Battalion and played a leading part in the operations against Gavrelle, taking the mayor's house (which was the key to the position) by assault and capturing the German garrison. It was largely due to him that Gavrelle was taken; and he was awarded a bar to his D.S.O.

In October, 1917, in the Battle of Passchendaele the Naval Division were heavily engaged. The following account of what happened near Poelcappelle (October 26th) is taken from the *History of the Royal Naval Division,* by Sub-Lieutenants Fry and McMillan:

On account of the serious losses in officers, the four battalions were getting out of hand when Commander Asquith, like the born fighter that he is, came forward and saved the situation. He placed his battalion in the most advantageous positions to meet any counter-attacks that might develop. That done, in spite of heavy artillery and machine-gun fire, he passed from end to end of the line we were holding and superintended the consolidation of our gains. In addition, he established liaison with the Canadians on our right, and thus closed a breach which might have caused us infinite trouble and been the source of our undoing.

Arthur Asquith was recommended for the V.C. (he, in fact, received a second bar to his D.S.O.); and these are the terms of the official recommendation:

Near Poelcappelle, during the operations of October 26th-27th, 1917, Commander Asquith displayed the greatest bravery, initiative and splendid leadership, and by his reconnaissance of the front line made under heavy fire, contributed much valuable information which made the successful continuance of the operations possible. During the morning of the 26th, when no news was forthcoming of the position of the attacking troops, Commander Asquith went forward, through heavy fire, round the front positions, and heedless of personal danger, found out our dispositions, got into touch with the troops on the right, and returned after some hours with most valuable information. On the night of the same day, he went forward alone in bright moonlight and explored the ground in the vicinity of Varlet Farm, where the situation was not clear. He was observed by the enemy, but, in spite of heavy rifle and machine-gun fire directed at him, and the fact that the going was necessarily slow, owing to the awful state of the ground, he approached Varlet Farm then reported to be in the hands of the enemy. Entering a concrete building alone he found it occupied by a small British garrison, who were exhausted and almost without ammunition and the most of them wounded. After investigating the ground thoroughly he returned and led up three platoons of a company of this battalion and relieved the garrison. He superintended the disposal of the troops, putting one platoon in the building as garrison and placing the other two platoons on each flank. A very important position was therefore kept entirely in our hands, owing to magnificent bravery, leadership and utter disregard of his own personal safety. This example of bravery and cool courage displayed throughout the operations by Commander Asquith encouraged the men to greater efforts, and kept up their moral. His valuable reconnaissance, the manner in which he led his men and his determination to hold the ground gained, contributed very largely to the success of the operations.

On December 16th, 1917, he was appointed Brigadier to command the 189th Brigade; and a few days later, in reconnoitring the position, he was again severely wounded. His leg had to be amputated and he was disabled from further active service in the war.

I never saw Arthur Asquith lose his temper or think of himself in my life.

.    .    .    .    .    .    .

I look around to see what child of which friend is left to become the wife of my son Anthony; and I wonder whether she will be as virtuous, loving and good-looking as my other daughters-in-law.

We were all wonderfully happy together, but, looking back, I think I was far from clever with my stepchildren; they grew up good and successful independently of me.

In consequence of our unpopularity in Peeblesshire, I had no opportunity of meeting other young people in their homes; and I knew no family except my own. The wealth of art and music, the luxury of flowers and colour, the stretches of wild country both in Scotland and high Leicestershire, which had made up my life till I married, had not qualified me to understand children reared in different circumstances. I would not perhaps have noticed many trifles in my step-family, had I not been so much made of, so overloved, caressed and independent before my marriage.

Every gardener prunes the roots of a tree before it is transplanted, but no one had ever pruned me. If you have been sunned through and through like an apricot on a wall from your earliest days, you are over-sensitive to any withdrawal of heat. This had been clearly foreseen by my friends and they were genuinely anxious about the happiness and future of my stepchildren. I do not know which of us had been considered the boldest in our marriage, my husband or myself; and no doubt step-relationships should not be taken in hand unadvisedly, lightly, or wantonly, but reverently, discreetly, and soberly. In every one of the letters congratulating me there had been a note of warning.

Mr. Gladstone wrote:

*May 5th,* 1894.
You have a great and noble work to perform. It is a work far beyond human strength. May the strength which is more than human be abundantly granted you.

Ever yours,
W. E. G.

I remember, on receiving this, saying to my beloved friend, Con Manners:

"Gladstone thinks my fitness to be Henry's wife should be prayed for like the clergy: 'Almighty and Everlasting God, who alone workest great marvels. . . .' "

John Morley wrote:

95 ELM PARK GARDENS,
SOUTH KENSINGTON,
S.W.
*March 7,* 1894.

MY DEAR MISS MARGOT,
Now that the whirl of congratulations must be ceasing, here are mine, the latest but not the least warm of them all. You are going to marry one of the finest men in all the world, with a great store of sterling gifts both of head and heart, and with a life before him of the highest interest, importance and

power. Such a man is a companion that any woman might envy you. I daresay you know this without my telling you. On the other part, I will not add myself to those impertinents who—as I understand you to report—wish you "to improve." I very respectfully wish nothing of the sort. Few qualities are better worth leaving as they are than vivacity, wit, freshness of mind, gaiety and pluck. Pray keep them all. Don't improve by an atom.

Circumstances may have a lesson or two to teach you, but 'tis only the dull who don't learn, and I have no fear but that such a pair have happy years in front of them.

You ask for my blessing and you have it. Be sure that I wish you as unclouded a life as can be the lot of woman, and I hope you will always let me count myself your friend. I possess some aphorisms on the married state—but they will keep. I only let them out as occasion comes.

Always yours sincerely,<br>JOHN MORLEY.

. . . . . . .

Looking back now on the first years of my marriage, I cannot exaggerate the gratitude which I feel for the tolerance, patience and loyalty that my stepchildren extended to a stranger; for, although I introduced an enormous amount of fun, beauty and movement into their lives, I could not replace what they had lost.

Henry's first wife, Helen Asquith, was an exceptionally pretty, refined woman; never dull, never artificial, and of single-minded goodness; she was a wonderful wife and a devoted mother, but was without illusions and even less adventurous than her children. She told me in one of our talks how much she regretted that her husband had taken silk and was in the House of Commons, at which I said in a glow of surprise:

"But surely, Mrs. Asquith, you are ambitious for your husband! Why, he's a *wonderful* man!"

This conversation took place in Grosvenor Square the second time that we met, when she brought her little girl to see me. Violet was aged four and a self-possessed, plump, clever little creature, with lovely hair hanging in Victorian ringlets down her back.

The children were not like Helen Asquith in appearance, except Raymond, who had her beautiful eyes and brow; but, just as they had none of their father's emotion and some of his intellect, they all inherited their mother's temperament, with the exception of Violet, who was more susceptible to the new environment than her brothers. The greatest compliment that was ever paid to my appearance—and one that helped me most when I felt discouraged in my early married life—was what Helen Asquith said to my husband and he repeated to me:

"There is something a little noble about Margot Tennant's expression."

.    .    .    .    .    .    .

If my stepchildren were patient with me, I dare not say what their father was: there are some reservations the boldest biographer has a right to claim; and I shall only write of my husband's character— his loyalty, lack of vanity, freedom from self, warmth and width of sympathy—in connection with politics and not with myself; but since I have touched on this subject I will give one illustration of his nature.

When the full meaning of the disreputable General Election of 1918, with its promises and pretensions and all its silly and false cries, was burnt into me at Paisley in this year of 1920 by our Coalition opponent re-repeating them, I said to Henry:

"Oh, if I had only quietly dropped all my friends of German name when the war broke out and never gone to say good-bye to those poor Lichnowskys, these ridiculous lies propagated entirely for political purposes would never have been told; and this criminal pro-German stunt could not have been started."

To which he replied:

"God forbid! I would rather ten thousand times be out of public life for ever."

# CHAPTER VII

VISIT TO WOMAN'S PRISON—INTERVIEW THERE WITH
MRS. MAYBRICK—SCENE IN A LIFER'S CELL; THE
HUSBAND WHO NEVER KNEW THOUGHT WIFE
MADE MONEY SEWING—MARGOT'S PLEA THAT
FAILED

MY husband was Home Secretary when we
married, and took a serious interest in our
prison system, which he found far from satis-
factory. He thought that it would be a good thing,
before we were known by sight, to pay a surprise
visit to the convict-prisons and that, if I could see
the women convicts and he could see the men
privately, he would be able to examine the conditions under which they served their sentences better
than if we were to go officially.

I was expecting my baby in about three months
when we made this expedition.

Wormwood Scrubs was the promising, almost
Dickens-like name of one of our convict-prisons
and, at that time, took in both men and women.

The governor scrutinised Henry's fine writing on

our permits; he received us dryly, but without suspicion; and we divided off, having settled to meet at the front door after an hour and a half's inspection.

The matron who accompanied me was a powerful, intelligent-looking woman of hard countenance and short speech. I put a few stupid questions to her about the prison: how many convicts they had, if the food was good, etc.

She asked me if I would care to see Mrs. Maybrick, an American criminal, who had been charged with murder, but sentenced for manslaughter. This woman had poisoned her husband with mild insistence by arsenic, but, as he was taking this for his health at the time of his death, the evidence was conflicting as to where he stopped and she began. She had the reputation of being a lady and beautiful; and petitions for her reprieve were sent to us signed by every kind of person from the United States. I told the matron I would see her and was shown into her cell, where I found her sitting on a stool against a bleak desk, at which she was reading. I noted her fine eyes and common mouth and, apologising, said:

"I hope you will not mind a stranger coming to

enquire how you are getting on," adding, "Have you any complaints to make of the prison?"

The matron had left me and, the doors being thick, I felt pretty sure she could not hear what we were saying.

MRS. MAYBRICK (*shrugging her shoulders*): "The butter here is abominable and we are only given two books—*The Pilgrim's Progress* and the Bible—and what do you say to our looking-glasses?" (*pointing to a little glass, four inches big, in a deep thick frame hanging on a peg*). "Do you know why it is so small?"

MARGOT: "No."

MRS. MAYBRICK: "Because the women who want to kill themselves can't get their heels in to break the glass; if they could they would cut their throats. The men don't have looking-glasses at all."

MARGOT: "Do you think they would like to have them?"

MRS. MAYBRICK (*shrugging her shoulders again and fingering her blue cotton blouse*): "I don't suppose they care! I'm sure no one could wish to see themselves with cropped hair and in these hideous clothes."

MARGOT: "I think that I could get you every

kind of book, if you like reading, and will tell me what you want."

MRS. MAYBRICK (*with a sudden laugh and looking at me with a contemptuous expression which made my heart ache*): "Oh, no, you couldn't! Never mind me! But you might tell them about the butter."

.    .    .    .    .    .    .

I did not find Mrs. Maybrick *sympathique* and shortly after this rejoined the matron. It was the first time I had seen a prison and my heart and mind were moved as we went from cell to cell nodding to the grey occupants.

"Have you any very bad cases?" I asked. "I mean any woman who is difficult and unhappy?"

MATRON: "Yes, there is one woman here who has been sitting on the floor for the last three days and, except a little water, I don't think she has swallowed a mouthful of food since she came in. She is a violent person and uses foul language. I do not think you had better see her."

MARGOT: "Thank you, I am not at all afraid. Please take me to her cell."

MATRON (*still reluctant and eyeing my figure*): "She may not speak to you, but if she does it might

MARGOT ASQUITH AND HER SON, ANTHONY, WHOSE INFLUENCE
OVER HER, SHE SAYS IN HER DIARY, HAS BEEN GREATER
THAN THAT OF ANY OTHER HUMAN BEING

give you a shock. Do you think you are wise to go in your present condition?"

MARGOT: "Oh, that's all right, thanks! I am not easily shocked."

When we came to the cell, I took the precaution of telling the matron she could leave me, as after this visit I should have to join my husband and I could find my way to the front hall by myself. She opened the door in silence and let me in.

Crouching on the stone floor, in an animal attitude, I saw a woman. She did not look up when I went in nor turn when I shut the door. Her eyebrows almost joined above a square-tipped nose; and her eyes, shaded by long black lashes, were fixed upon the ground. Her hair grew well, out of a beautiful forehead, and the red curve of her mouth gave expression to a wax-like face. I had never seen a more striking-looking creature.

After my usual apology and a gentle recitative of why I had come, she turned what little I could see of her face away from me and whatever I suggested after that was greeted with impenetrable silence.

At last I said to her:

"It is so difficult for me to stand and talk while

[241]

you are sitting on the ground. Won't you get up?"

No answer. At this—being an active woman—I sat down beside her on the stone floor and took her hand in both of mine. She did not withdraw it, but lifted her lashes to look at me. I noted the sullen, exhausted expression in her grey eyes; my heart beat at the beauty of her face.

"Why don't you speak to me?" I said. "I might, for all you know, be able to do a great deal for you."

This was greeted by a faint gleam and a prolonged shake of the head.

MARGOT: "You look very young. What is it you did, that brought you into this prison,"

My question seemed to surprise her and after a moment's silence she said:

"Don't you know why I am sentenced?"

MARGOT: "No; and you need not tell me if you don't want to. How long are you here for?"

THE WOMAN (*in a penetrating voice*): "Life!"

MARGOT: "That's impossible; no one is punished for life unless they commit murder; and even then the sentence is always shortened."

THE WOMAN: "Shortened in time for what? For your death and burial? Perhaps you don't

[242]

HOME SECRETARIES: PAST AND PRESENT DOWN TO H. H. ASQUITH

[243]

know how kind they are to us here! No one is allowed to die in prison! But by the time your health is gone, your hair white and your friends are dead, your family do not need you and all that can be done for you is done by charity. You die and your eyes are closed by your landlady."

MARGOT: "Tell me what you did."

THE WOMAN: "Only what all you fashionable women do every day. . . ."

MARGOT: "What?"

THE WOMAN: "I helped those who were in trouble to get rid of their babies."

MARGOT: "Did you take money for it?"

THE WOMAN: "Sometimes I did it for nothing."

MARGOT: "What sort of women did you help?"

THE WOMAN: "Oh, quite poor women!"

MARGOT: "When you charged them, how much money did you ask for?"

THE WOMAN: "Four or five pounds and often less."

MARGOT: "Was your husband a respectable man and did he know anything about it?"

THE WOMAN: "My husband was highly respected. He was a stone-mason, and well to do,

[245]

and knew nothing at all till I was arrested. . . .
He thought I made money sewing."

MARGOT: "Poor man, how tragic!"

After this rather stupid ejaculation of mine, she
relapsed into a frozen silence and I got up off the
ground and asked her if she liked books. No answer. If the food was good? No answer. If her
bed was clean and comfortable? But all my questions were in vain. At last she broke the silence by
saying:

"You said just now that you might be able to
help me. There is only one thing in the world that
I want, and you could not help to get it. . . . No
one can help me. . . ."

MARGOT: "Tell me what you want. How can I
or any one else help you while you sit on the ground,
neither speaking nor eating? Get up and I will
listen to you; otherwise I shall go away."

After this she got up stiffly and lifted her arms in
a stretch above her head, showing the outline of her
fine bust. I said to her:

"I would like to help you."

THE WOMAN: "I want to see one person and
only one. I think of nothing else and wonder night
and day how it could be managed."

[246]

MARGOT: "Tell me who it is, this one person, that you think of and want so much to see."

THE WOMAN: "I want to see Mrs. Asquith."

MARGOT (*dumb with surprise*): "Why?"

THE WOMAN: "Because she is only just married and will never again have as much influence over her husband as she has now; and I am told she is kind. . . ."

MARGOT (*moving towards her*): "I am Mrs. Asquith."

At this the woman gave a sort of howl and, shivering, with her teeth set, flung herself at my feet and clasped my ankles with an iron clutch. I should have fallen, but, loosening her hold with great rapidity, she stood up and, facing me, held me by my shoulders. The door opened and the matron appeared, at which the woman sprang at her with a tornado of oaths, using strange words that I had never heard before. I tried to silence her, but in vain, so I told the matron that she might go and find out if my husband was ready for me. She did not move and seemed put out by my request.

"I really think," she said, "that you are extremely foolish risking anything with this woman."

THE WOMAN (*in a penetrating voice*): "You

clear out and go to hell with you! This person is a Christian, and you are not! You are a —— —— !"

I put my hand over her mouth and said I would leave her for ever if she did not stop swearing. She sat down. I turned to the matron and said:

"You need not fear for me, thank you; we prefer being left alone."

When the matron had shut the door, the woman sprang up and, banging it with her back, remained with arms akimbo and her legs apart, looking at me in defiance. I thought to myself, as I watched her resolute face and strong, young figure, that, if she wanted to prevent me getting out of that room alive, she could easily do so.

THE WOMAN: "You heard what I said, that you would never have as much influence with your husband as you have now, so just listen. He is all-powerful and, if he looks into my case, he will see that I am innocent and ought to be let out. The last Home Secretary was not married and never took any interest in us poor women."

Hearing the matron tapping at the door and feeling rather anxious to get out, I said:

"I give you my word of honour that I will make my husband read up all your case. The matron will give me your name and details, but I must go now."

THE WOMAN (*with a sinister look*): "Oh, no, you don't! You stay here till *I* give you the details: what does a woman like that care for a woman like me?" (*throwing her thumb over her shoulder towards the matron behind the door*). "What does she know about life?"

MARGOT: "You must let me open the door and get a pencil and paper."

THE WOMAN: "The old lady will do it for you while I give you the details of my case. You have only got to give her your orders. Does she know who you are?"

MARGOT: "No; and you must not tell her, please. If you will trust me with your secret, I will trust you with mine; but you must let me out first if I am to help you."

With a lofty wave of my hand, but without taking one step forward, I made her move away from the door, which I opened with a feeling of relief. The matron was in the passage and, while she was fetching a pencil, the woman, standing in the doorway of her cell, told me in lowered tones how cruelly unlucky she had been in life; what worthless, careless girls had passed through her hands; and how they had died from no fault of hers, but through their own ignorance. She ended by saying:

"There is no gratitude in this world. . . ."

When the matron came back, she was much shocked at seeing me kiss the convict.

I said, "Good-bye," and never saw her again.

My husband looked carefully into her case, but found that she was a professional abortionist of the most hopeless type.

# CHAPTER VIII

SIR JOHN WILLIAMS* was my doctor and would have been a remarkable man in any country, but in Wales he was unique. He was a man of heart without hysteria and both loyal and truthful.

On the 18th of May, 1895, my sisters Charlotte and Lucy were sitting with me in my bedroom. I will quote from my diary the account of my first confinement and how I got to know him:

"I began to feel ill. My Gamp, an angular-faced, admirable old woman called Jerusha Taylor —'out of the Book of Kings'—was bustling about preparing for the doctor. Henry was holding my hands and I was sobbing in an arm-chair, feeling

*Sir John Williams, of Aberystwyth, Wales.

the panic of pain and fear which no one can realise who has not had a baby.

"When Williams arrived, I felt as if salvation must be near; my whole soul and every beat of my heart went out in dumb appeal to him, and his tenderness on that occasion bred in me a love and gratitude which never faded, but was intensified by all I saw of him afterwards. He seemed to think a narcotic would calm my nerves, but the sleeping-draught might have been water for all the effect it had upon me, so he gave me chloroform. The room grew dark; grey poppies appeared to be nodding at me—and I gasped:

" 'Oh, doctor, *dear* doctor, stay with me to-night, just *this* one night, and I will stay with you whenever you like!'

"But Williams was too anxious, my nurse told me, to hear a word I said.

"At four o'clock in the morning, Henry went to fetch the anæsthetist and in his absence Williams took me out of chloroform. Then I seemed to have a glimpse of a different world: if *pain* is evil, then it was *hell;* if not, I expect I got nearer Heaven than I have ever been before. . . .

"I saw Dr. Bailey at the foot of the bed, with a

bag in his hand, and Charty's outline against the lamp; then my head was placed on the pillow and a black thing came between me and the light and closed over my mouth, a slight beating of carpets sounded in my brain and I knew no more. . . .

"When I came to consciousness about twelve the next morning, I saw Charty looking at me and I said to her in a strange voice:

" 'I can't have any more pain, it's no use.'

"CHARTY: 'No, no, darling, you won't have any more.' (*Silence.*)

"MARGOT: 'But you don't mean it's all over?'

"CHARTY (*soothingly*): 'Go to sleep, dearest.'

"I was so dazed by chloroform that I could hardly speak. Later on the nurse told me that the doctor had had to sacrifice my baby and that I ought to be grateful for being spared, as I had had a very dangerous confinement.

"When Sir John Williams came to see me, he looked white and tired and, finding my temperature was normal, he said fervently:

" 'Thank you, Mrs. Asquith.'

"I was too weak and uncomfortable to realise all that had happened; and what I suffered from the smallest noise I can hardly describe. I would

watch nurse slowly approaching and burst into a
perspiration when her cotton dress crinkled against
the chintz of my bed. I shivered with fear when
the blinds were drawn up or the shutters unfast-
ened; and any one moving up or down stairs, placing a tumbler on the marble wash-hand-stand or
reading a newspaper would bring tears into my
eyes."

In connection with what I have quoted out of
my diary here it is not inappropriate to add that I
lost my babies in three out of my five confinements.
These poignant and secret griefs have no place on
the high-road of life; but, just as Henry and I will
stand sometimes side by side near those little graves
unseen by strangers, so he and I in unobserved moments will touch with one heart an unforgotten
sorrow.

Out of the many letters which I received, this
from our intimate and affectionate friend, Lord
Haldane, was the one I liked best:

My dear Friend,
    I cannot easily tell you how much touched I was
in the few minutes I spent talking to you this afternoon, by what I saw and what you told me. I left
with the sense of witnessing triumph in failure and
life come through death. The strength that is given

at such times arises not from ignoring loss, or persuading oneself that the thing is not that *is;* but from the resolute setting of the face to the East and the taking of one step onwards. It is the quality we touch—it may be but for a moment—not the quantity we have, that counts. "All I could never be, all that was lost in me is yet there—in His hand who planned the perfect whole." That was what Browning saw vividly when he wrote his Rabbi Ben Ezra. You have lost a great joy. But in the deepening and strengthening the love you two have for each other you have gained what is rarer and better; it is well worth the pain and grief—the grief you have borne in common—and you will rise stronger and freer.

We all of us are parting from youth, and the horizon is narrowing, but I do not feel any loss that is not compensated by gain, and I do not think that you do either. Anything that detaches one, that makes one turn from the past and look simply at what one has to do, brings with it new strength and new intensity of interest. I have no fear for you when I see what is absolutely and unmistakably good and noble obliterating every other thought as I saw it this afternoon. I went away with strengthened faith in what human nature was capable of.

May all that is highest and best lie before you both.

Your affec. friend,
R. B. HALDANE.

I was gradually recovering my health when on May the 21st, 1895, after an agonising night, Sir John Williams and Henry came into my bedroom between five and six in the morning and I was told that I should have to lie on my back till August, as I was suffering from phlebitis; but I was too unhappy and disappointed to mind. It was then that my doctor, Sir John Williams, became my friend as well as my nurse, and his nobility of character made him a powerful influence in my life.

To return to my diary:

"Queen Victoria took a great interest in my confinement, and wrote Henry a charming letter. She sent messengers constantly to ask after me and I answered her myself once, in pencil, when Henry was at the Home Office.

"I was convalescing one day, lying as usual on my bed, my mind a blank, when Sir William Harcourt's card was sent up to me and my door was darkened by his huge form.

I had seen most of my political and other friends while I was convalescing: Mr. Gladstone, Lord Haldane, Mr. Birrell, Lord Spencer, Lord Rosebery, the Archbishop of Canterbury, John Morley, Arthur Balfour, Sir Alfred Lyall and

Admiral Maxse; and I was delighted to see Sir William Harcourt. When he came into my room, he observed my hunting-crops hanging on the wall from a rack, and said:

"I am glad to see those whips! Asquith will be able to beat you if you play fast and loose with him. That little tight mouth of his convinces me he has the capacity to do it.

"After my nurse had left the room, he expressed surprise that I should have an ugly woman near me, however good she might be, and told me that his son, Bobby, had been in love with his nurse and wrote to her for several years. He added, in his best Hanoverian vein:

" 'I encourage my boys all I can in this line; it promises well for their future.' "

"After some talk, Mr. John Morley's card was brought up and, seeing Sir William look rather subdued, I told the servant to ask him to wait in my boudoir for a few minutes and assured my guest that I was in no hurry for him to go; but Harcourt began to fidget about and after a little he insisted on John Morley coming up. We had a good talk *à trois,* starting by abusing men who minded other people's opinion or what the newspapers said of

[257]

them. Knowing, as I did, that both of them were highly sensitive to the Press, I encouraged the conversation.

"JOHN MORLEY: 'I can only say I agree with what Joe once said to me, "I would rather the newspapers were for than against me." '

"SIR WILLIAM: 'My dear chap, you would surely not rather have the *Daily Chronicle* on your side. Why, bless my soul, our party has had more harm done it through the *Daily Chronicle* than anything else!'

"MARGOT: 'Do you think so? I think its screams, though pitched a little high, are effective!'

"JOHN MORLEY: 'Oh, you like Massingham, of course, because your husband is one of his heroes.'

"SIR WILLIAM: 'Well, all I can say is he always abuses me and I am glad of it.'

"JOHN MORLEY: 'He abuses me, too, though not, perhaps, quite so often as you!'

"MARGOT: 'I would like him to praise me. I think his descriptions of the House of Commons debates are not only true and brilliant but fine literature; there is both style and edge in his writing and I rather like that bitter-almond flavour! How strangely the paper changed over to Lord Rosebery, didn't it?'

"Feeling this was ticklish ground, as Harcourt thought that he and not Rosebery should have been Prime Minister, I turned the talk on to Goschen.

"Sir William: 'It is sad to see the way Goschen has lost his hold in the country; he has not been at all well treated by his colleagues.'

"This seemed to me to be also rather risky, so I said boldly that I thought Goschen had done wonders in the House and country, considering he had a poor voice and was naturally cautious. I told them I loved him personally and that Jowett at whose house I first met him shared my feeling in valuing his friendship. After this he took his departure, promising to bring me roses from Malwood.

"John Morley—the most fastidious and fascinating of men—stayed on with me and suggested quite seriously that, when we went out of office (which might happen any day), he and I should write a novel together. He said that, if I would write the plot and do the female characters, he would manage the men and politics.

I asked if he wanted the old Wilkie Collins idea of a plot with a hundred threads drawn into one woof, or did he prefer modern nothingness, a shred of a story attached to unending analysis and the infinitely little commented upon with elaborate and pretentious humour. He scorned the latter.

I asked him if he did not want to go permanently away from politics to literature and discussed all his wonderful books and writings. I chaffed him about the way he had spoken of me before our marriage, in spite of the charming letter he had written, how it had been repeated to me that he had said my light-hearted indiscretions would ruin Henry's career; and I asked him what I had done since to merit his renewed confidence.

"He did not deny having criticised me, for although 'Honest John'—the name by which he went among the Radicals—was singularly ill-chosen, I never heard of Morley telling a lie. He was quite impenitent and I admired his courage.

"After an engrossing conversation, every moment of which I loved, he said good-bye to me and I leant back against the pillow and gazed at the pattern on the wall.

"Henry came into my room shortly after this and told me the Government had been beaten by seven in a vote of censure passed on Campbell-Bannerman in Supply, in connection with small arms ammunition. I looked at him wonderingly and said:

" 'Are you sad, darling, that we are out?'

"To which he replied:

" 'Only for one reason. I wish I had completed my prison reforms. I have, however, appointed the best committee ever seen, who will go on with my work. Ruggles-Brise, the head of it, is a splendid little fellow!'

"At that moment he received a note to say he was wanted in the House of Commons immediately, as Lord Rosebery had been sent for by the Queen. This excited us much and, before he could finish telling me what had happened, he went straight down to Westminster. . . . John Morley had missed this fateful division, as he was sitting with me, and Harcourt had only just arrived at the House in time to vote.

"Henry returned at 1 a.m. and came to say good night to me: he generally said his prayers by my bedside. He told me that St. John Brodrick's motion to reduce C. B.'s salary by £100 had turned the

Government out; that Rosebery had resigned and gone straight down to Windsor; that Campbell-Bannerman was indignant and hurt; that few of our men were in the House; and that Akers Douglas, the Tory Whip, could not believe his eyes when he handed the figures to Tom Ellis, our chief Whip, who returned them to him in silence.

"The next morning St. John Brodrick came to see me, full of excitement and sympathy. He was anxious to know if we minded his being instrumental in our downfall; but I am so fond of him that, of course, I told him that I did not mind, as a week sooner or later makes no difference and St. John's division was only one out of many indications in the House and the country that our time was up. Henry came back from the Cabinet in the middle of our talk and shook his fist in fun at 'our enemy.' He was tired, but good-humoured as ever.

"At 3.30 Princess Hélène d'Orléans came to see me and told me of her engagement to the Duc d'Aosta. She looked tall, black and distinguished. She spoke of Prince Eddy to me with great frankness. I told her I had sometimes wondered at her devotion to one less clever than herself. At this her eyes filled with tears and she explained to me how much she had been in love and the sweetness and nobility of his character. I had reason to know the truth of what she said when one day Queen Alexandra, after talking to me in moving terms of her dead son, wrote in my Prayer Book:

"Man looketh upon the countenance, but God upon the heart.

"Hélène adores the Princess of Wales* but not the Prince!† and says the latter's rudeness to her brother, the Duc d'Orléans, is terrible. I said nothing, as I am devoted to the Prince and think her brother deserves any ill-treatment he gets. I asked her if she was afraid of the future: a new country and the prospect of babies, etc. She answered that d'Aosta was so genuinely devoted that it would make everything easy for her.

" 'What would you do if he were unfaithful to you?' I asked.

"PRINCESS HÉLÈNE: 'Oh! I told Emanuel. . . . I said, "You see? I leave you. . . . If you are not true to me, I instantly leave you," and I should do so at once.'

*Queen Alexandra.
†King Edward VII.

"She begged me never to forget her, but always to pray for her.

" 'I love you,' she said, 'as every one else does'; and with a warm embrace she left the room.

"She came of a handsome family: Blowitz's famous description, *'de loin on dirait un Prussien, de près un imbécile,'* was made of a near relation of the Duchesse d'Aosta."

．　．　．　．　．　．　．

With the fall of the Government my diary of that year ceases to have the smallest interest.

# CHAPTER IX

MARGOT IN 1906 SUMS UP HER LIFE; A LOT OF LOVE-MAKING, A LITTLE FAME AND MORE ABUSE—A REAL MAN AND GREAT HAPPINESS

I WILL finish with a character-sketch of myself copied out of my diary, written nine weeks before the birth of my fifth and last baby in 1906, and like everything else that I have quoted never intended for the public eye:

"I am not pretty, and I do not know anything about my expression, although I observe it is this that is particularly dwelt upon if one is sufficiently plain; but I hope, when you feel as kindly towards your fellow-creatures as I do, that some of that warmth may modify an otherwise bright and rather knifey *contour*.

"My figure has remained as it was: slight, well-balanced and active. Being socially courageous and not at all shy, I think I can come into a room as well as many people of more appearance and prestige. I do not propose to treat myself like Mr. Bernard Shaw in this account. I shall neither excuse myself from praise, nor shield myself from blame, but put down the figures as accurately as I can and leave others to add them up.

"I think I have imagination, born not of fancy, but of feeling; a conception of the beautiful, not merely in poetry, music, art and nature, but in human beings. I have insight into human nature, derived not only from a courageous experience, but also from imagination; and I have a clear thoug distant vision, down dark, long and often diverge t avenues, of the ordered meaning of God. I t ke this opportunity of saying my religion is a vibra ng reality never away from me; and this is all I hall write upon the subject.

"It is difficult to describe what one me ns by imagination, but I think it is more than in entiveness, or fancy. I remember discussing the question with John Addington Symonds and, to gi e him a hasty illustration of what I meant, I said I thought naming a Highland regiment 'The Blac Watch' showed a *high* degree of imagination. He was pleased with this; and as a personal tes imonial I may add that both he and Jowett told ne that no one could be as good a judge of charact r as I was

[266]

who was without imagination. In an early love-
letter to me, Henry wrote:

"Imaginative insight you have more than any one
I have ever met!

I think I am deficient in one form of imagination; and Henry will agree with this. I have a
great longing to help those I love: this leads me to
intrepid personal criticism; and I do not always
know what hurts my friends' feelings. I do not
think I should mind anything that I have said to
others being said to me, but one never can tell; I
have a good, sound digestion and personally prefer
knowing the truth; I have taken adverse criticism
pretty well all my life and had a lot of it; but by
some gap I have not succeeded in making my friends
take it well. I am not vain or touchy; it takes a lot
to offend me; but when I am hurt the scar remains.
I feel differently about people who have hurt me;
my confidence has been shaken; I hope I am not
ungenerous, but I fear I am not really forgiving.
Worldly people say that explanations are a mistake; but having it out is the only chance any one
can ever have of retaining my love; and those who
have neither the courage, candour nor humbleness

to say they are wrong are not worth loving. I am not afraid of suffering too much in life, but much more afraid of feeling too little; and quarrels make me profoundly unhappy. One of my complaints against the shortness of life is that there is not time enough to feel pity and love for enough people. I am infinitely compassionate and moved to my foundations by the misfortunes of other people.

"As I said in my 1888 character-sketch, truthfulness with me is hardly a virtue, but I cannot discriminate between truths that need and those that need not be told. Want of courage is what makes so many people lie. It would be difficult for me to say exactly what I am afraid of. Physically and socially not much; morally, I am afraid of a good many things: reprimanding servants, bargaining in shops; or to turn to more serious matters, the loss of my health, the children's or Henry's. Against these last possibilities I pray in every recess of my thoughts.

"With becoming modesty I have said that I am imaginative, loving and brave! What then are my faults?

"I am fundamentally nervous, impatient, irritable and restless. These may sound slight shortcomings, but they go to the foundation of my nature, crippling my activity, lessening my influence and preventing my achieving anything remarkable. I wear myself out in a hundred unnecessary ways, regretting the trifles I have not done, arranging and re-arranging what I have got to do and what every one else is going to do, till I can hardly eat or sleep. To be in one position for long at a time, or sit through bad plays, to listen to moderate music or moderate conversation is a positive punishment to me. I am energetic and industrious, but I am a little too quick; I am *driven* along by my temperament till I tire myself and every one else.

"I did not marry till I was thirty. This luckily gave me time to read; and I collected nearly a thousand books of my own before I married. If I had had real application—as all the Asquiths have—I should by now be a well-educated woman; but this I never had. I am not at all dull, and never stale, but I don't seem to be able to grind at uncongenial things. I have a good memory for books and conversations, but bad for poetry and dates; wonderful for faces and pitiful for names.

"Physically I have done pretty well for myself.

I ride better than most people and have spent or wasted more time on it than any woman of intellect ought to.  I have broken both collar-bones, all my ribs and my knee-cap; dislocated my jaw, fractured my skull, gashed my nose and had five concussions of the brain; but—though my horses are to be sold next week*—I have not lost my nerve.  I dance, drive and skate well; I don't skate very well, but I dance really well.  I have a talent for drawing and am intensely musical, playing the piano with a touch of the real thing, but have neglected both these accomplishments.  I may say here in self-defence that marriage and five babies, five step-children and a husband in high politics have all contributed to this neglect, but the root of the matter lies deeper: I am restless.

"After riding, what I have enjoyed doing most in my life is writing.  I have written a great deal, but do not fancy publishing my exercises.  I have always kept a diary and commonplace books and for many years I wrote criticisms of everything I read.  It is rather difficult for me to say what I think of my own writing.  Arthur Balfour once

*My horses were sold at Tattersalls, June 11th, 1906.

said that I was the best letter-writer he knew; Henry tells me I write well; and Symonds said I had *l'oreille juste;* but writing of the kind that I like reading I cannot do: it is a long apprenticeship. Possibly, if I had had this apprenticeship forced upon me by circumstances, I should have done it better than anything else. I am a careful critic of all I read and I do not take my opinions of books from other people; I have not got 'a lending-library mind' as Henry well described that of a friend of ours. I do not take my opinions upon anything from other people; from this point of view—not a very high one—I might be called original.

"When I read Arthur Balfour's books and essays, I realised before I had heard them discussed what a beautiful style he wrote. Raymond, whose intellectual taste is as fine as his father's, wrote in a paper for his All Souls Fellowship that Arthur had the finest style of any living writer; and Raymond and Henry often justify my literary verdicts.

"From my earliest age I have been a collector: not of anything particularly valuable, but of letters, old photographs of the family, famous people and odds and ends. I do not lose things. Our cigarette ash-trays are plates from my dolls' dinner-service; I have got china, books, whips, knives, match-boxes and clocks given me since I was a small child. I have kept our early copy-books, with all the family signatures in them, and many trifling landmarks of nursery life. I am painfully punctual, tidy and methodical, detesting indecision, change of plans and the egotism that they involve. I am a little stern and severe except with children: for these I have endless elasticity and patience. Many of my faults are physical. If I could have chosen my own life—more in the hills and less in the traffic—I should have slept better and might have been less overwrought and disturbable. But after all I may improve, for I am on a man-of-war, as a friend once said to me, which is better than being on a pirate-ship and is a profession in itself.

"Well, I have finished; I have tried to relate of my manners, morals, talents, defects, temptations, and appearance as faithfully as I can; and I think there is nothing more to be said. If I had to confess and expose one opinon of myself which might differentiate me a little from other people, I should say it was my power of love coupled with my power of criticism, but what I lack most is what Henry possesses above all men: equanimity, moderation, self-control and the authority that comes from a perfect sense of proportion. I can only pray that I am not too old or too stationary to acquire these.

MARGOT ASQUITH.

"P.S. This is my second attempt to write about myself and I am not at all sure that my old character-sketch of 1888 is not the better of the two— it is more external—but, after all, what can one say of one's inner self that corresponds with what one really is or what one's friends think one is? Just now I am within a few weeks of my baby's birth and am tempted to take a gloomy view. I am inclined to sum up my life in this way:

" 'An unfettered childhood and triumphant youth; a lot of love-making and a little abuse; a little fame and more abuse; a real man and great happiness; the love of children and seventh heaven; an early death and a crowded memorial service.'

"But perhaps I shall not die, but live to write an-

[273]

other volume of this diary and a better description
of an improved self."

_Margot Asquith_

Begun at Littlestone-on-Sea,
June 1st, 1906, and finished at
Rothes in Scotland, August 5th,
in the same year.

**THE END**

# INDEX

## A

# INDEX

# INDEX

# INDEX

# INDEX

## L

## M

## N

## O

# INDEX

## P

## R

## S

# INDEX

# INDEX